Shattered Dreams

P.P. Jackson

No one lives and works as a Solitary Island,

we all influence other people in everything we do.

authorHOUSE®

AuthorHouse™ UK Ltd.
500 Avebury Boulevard
Central Milton Keynes, MK9 2BE
www.authorhouse.co.uk
Phone: 08001974150

First published by AuthorHouse   7/9/2010

ISBN: 978-1-4520-4394-4 (sc)

This book is printed on acid-free paper.

To my mother

Acknowledgements:

I would like to extend my appreciation to:

All those who helped me in compiling this book. Those who also gave me the courage to write this book. You definitely know yourselves, god bless you, and I will never thank you enough.

Contents

Introduction

Inasmuch as these are my lifetime experiences, I felt compelled to write them and share them with you. We all dream! When we are sad, we dream of a future filled with happiness. When the weather is cold and wet, we dream of warm days when the sun always shines. When we feel unwell we dream of being healthy and strong all our lives. When we are broke we dream of a future full of money, never mind where the money is going to come from! In addition, of course we dream of winning millions in the lottery and being able to shop until we drop.

Nowadays in my country, most ordinary people dream of things that people in the developed world take for granted, for example, being able to buy food, clothing and having a roof over their heads. Most people dream of being able to get a job so they can pay school fees for their children, pay for health care and look after their families and their extended families. Right at the back of their minds, they may dream of a day when they could afford luxuries like cars, electricity and telephones. These are dreams that they know will never come true in their lives. They stay in the very far unreachable distance.

Indeed, there was a time when life in my country was easier and as long as one worked hard, dreams used to come true. These are the so called 'good old days!' anyone, even the street vendors, could afford to pay for all the basic necessities of life plus a few more luxuries like big stereos, televisions and even cars. Other professionals like teachers and nurses could easily afford to buy houses in the suburban areas. Most households could afford to employ nannies, house cleaners, chefs and gardeners. In fact, all of this we took for granted.

I, like everyone else, had some dreams. As a young girl I dreamt of getting married to the richest man, I could find. That is because in the old days women were expected to get married, have babies and become housewives, I did not want to be selling fruits and vegetables at the market like my mother. In my teens, my dreams changed, I pushed the marriage dream to the further end of my twenties. I realised that if I worked hard enough at school I could do better than just getting married and producing babies. I decided that I wanted to become a professional model. I got this idea from the 'Parade' magazine and other international magazines. Towards the end of my high school years, my dreams changed. This was because of the promises of a better Zimbabwe where there would be better opportunities for all. I now dreamt of a profession in the financial institutions.

I dreamt of one day becoming an executive in the banking sector or even owning my own bank. Some years later, after working in one of the leading banks in the country, I discovered that my dream of being a banking executive let alone owning a bank was unachievable so my dreams changed. I left the country for Europe for a profession that would help me contribute to the development of the country. I thought this was a more challenging profession and that I could at least help my people. In fact, I decided that this was my final and last dream that promised the brightest and most exciting future that I had dreamt about for years and years. I was finally going to achieve my dreams!

Whatever dreams I had had from when I was only a little girl to when I became a young woman, they were all about being successful in whatever profession I would choose to pursue. One thing that I never dreamt of was leaving my country to settle in a foreign country with uncertain future! I never dreamt of working as a carer in an old people's home! I never dreamt of working in a hospital, let alone in a foreign country! My dreams have been shattered!

Blessed are those who have been able to achieve their dreams! In my country, people no longer 'dream!' they are too frightened of getting disappointed because dreams never come true. They just carry on their lives living each day as it comes. They have lost all hope for a brighter future. In fact, if they dream at all they always have nightmares about prices of basic items going up, dream about being beaten up by the police and about what other nightmares the government is planning for them!

As for me, I have given up dreaming! There is no point of dreaming anymore because I have no idea what the future holds for me. I am too afraid of dreaming. I just thank god that I am alive and can at least put food on my table every day.

As far as this book is concerned, it details the hidden stories of Africans, colour, race or creed, living in Europe. In any event, I never dreamt of politics, economic hardships to displace a whole people. My experiences have shown me however, that its perhaps not surprising, and I have come to realise that - in a split second, one can become homeless, with nothing to live on, and a refugee in another country.

I call them disasters, and these disasters are not natural, or neither uncontrollable. We have learned the hard way, there are two disasters both of them can cause a very hard impact on human nature. There are manmade disasters, which in certain instances can be avoidable; these are due to economical, political, and power hungry. I call them disasters because it is very sad in the cruel inhumane means that one endures to hang on to power certainly Zimbabwe has shown those disasters, which have lacked the respect for human dignity, life has become very difficult. History, of course, can demonstrate many such instances throughout the globe.

How easily people can become trapped in their our naivety - trusting people - believing that success is in the palms of their hands when - in reality - it was out of reach, due to political circumstances. One quickly learns from bitter experience that bureaucracy corruption can lead to the suffering, hunger of a given society.

In this case, there are certain issues that in life, you cannot avoid talking about one can no longer pretend that they are not affected. Heard that saying," **half the world is composed of people who have something to say and cant, other half, those who have nothing to say and keep on saying it.** Some of us are not part of the nothing to say brigade that is the main reason I have written this book. I have suffered in silence long enough I suppose!

This book is based on a true story – the lifetime journey of an African woman – me. I was born in Rhodesia I have a lot of township experience, growing up under the Rhodesian regime. I understand too well from firsthand experience the words 'racism' and 'segregation'.

My understanding of racism is the ignorance of a people not wanting to understand the religion and culture of people different from themselves. The people themselves can find many solutions. It is as easy as choosing a society's culture that one is comfortable with then learn about it – getting to know people will break down the barriers and misunderstanding that exists in the world these days. As Africans from the former British colonies we have many British mannerisms the way we are is still British oriented.

At a tender age I did swim in shit for my survival, others drowned. One cannot easily forget such experiences, forgive but never forget. I would like you to understand why we have come to your countries here in Europe.

This has been a clear demonstration that we did not agree with the current political, economical status of our country. This demonstration clearly showed that no matter how much one shouts or insults the international countries; we stood by them, the international countries. That is enough to understand our intention. We left, to show our solidarity. In Zimbabwe life is hard – no money – no food. We struggle to make ends meet but we will never get there just by working. Believe me it is not easy to watch your off springs perishing because just getting out of the country and doing whatever you can to contribute financially towards their future is not enough – but in your helplessness, you do whatever you are able to help them have a future. In addition, if that mean, leaving hearth and home – abandoning all you hold dear to work in another country – that is what you have to do. There is no alternative. That is what countless others and I have had to do. Moreover, believe me we have wept bitter tears in the process.

Life during Rhodesian Period

Chapter 1

They say a journey of a million miles begins with a single step. Well my journey of life began at an early age, when I started to understand my surroundings. Once upon a time, there was a country called Rhodesia, ruled by the British Empire, became Zimbabwe ruled by the black majority people. I was born in Rhodesia and I grew up during the Rhodesian period until I was a young woman. During this period, black people's life was just well for as long as you were working, had a roof over your head. However, as a black person there was always something about us that I started to realise when I was five years old. We were the low class. Mixed race people had a better class than us. Mixed race people where mostly in the Rhodesian army most of the mixed race women were government clerks working in offices. Other mixed race women were allowed to work in shops as shop assistants. They had their own dwelling areas, which had better living standards than the black Africans townships. Their dwelling areas where nearer to the town centres and nearer to the army barracks. They lived their life that was full of their own standards, fast cars, drinking until they drop big families.

Which under the proper observation one can come to conclusion that they were actually being used to fight the war against blacks and their life was not valued until some of the coloured people stated to move into the black owned accommodations, and started to support the black in their fight for human rights. They realised that it was cheap and affordable. . They had the support of the social services when they were out of work. Accommodation was practically located to them. These were their African-English grandchildren. Most of them perished during the course of the war. Nevertheless, those who remained and went to school properly they started to refuse to go to the war, and were now participating in the political scenario. They were welcome to come to the African townships. They learned to live with the blacks and started to relate well.

As for the Indian people, they kept to themselves as different people from blacks and all other races in Zimbabwe. They had their arranged marriages. They never socialised that much with other people. They were trading and they are the ones who hard paved their society's respect by offering their monies to buy land from the government to build their own houses out of town and away from the blacks, and nearer to the white Rhodesians. People of Indian origins were known for their business issues, and they never used the bank to bank their money that they accrued through their businesses. Indians were known to like black market business.

As for black Africans, its either they were housekeepers, cleaners, (chambermaids) hotel cleaners in hotels, gardeners, and all the dirty work you can think of. It was far too obvious there was no room for blacks. I remember in the sixties when there were demonstrations by the black Africans of Rhodesia trying to liberate themselves from segregation, they wanted equal rights and opportunities, be offered to all besides colour race or creed with their fellow white Rhodesians. In the townships of Rhodesia, now Zimbabwe we use to have our supper around four o'clock in the afternoon and go to bed before six o'clock in the evening. There was that restriction of movement in our townships. After a demonstration in the town centre, there would be no rest in our town ships that night and the (BSAP) British South African Police will come to mobilise blacks and beat them up for the demonstration. I remember vividly, my young sister was around two years, and I was a three year old. My mother use to ask me to play with her whilst she prepared our meals, she use to bath us together in a big bath bowl as I use to call it.

On this particular day, the mobilisation of black Africans was very serious, the beatings, humiliation was unbearable due to the demonstrations that ended up blacks burning shops in the town centre, Salisbury (now Harare). Every woman and every child was mobilised to go to the biggest police station, Harare, (now Mbare police station) was the police station for black people to be torched and humiliated. People had to walk for over ten miles, on foot at night. It was late at night and my mother told me not to let her hand go, if I cannot keep up, she told me to hold on to her skirt. She told me to follow her, wherever she decides to go, I could see that my mother was frightened to death, but she was so determined to do whatever for her survival, and her offspring's.

We were being mobilised to go through this small industrial contaminated sewage stream, which was pouring its dirty contaminated water, to sewage, nearby our township. My mother took advantage of the rain. She pulled me close to her and whispered we have to swim down towards the sewage. I did swim in the industrial shit, at a tender age of three.

We sat by this stream's banks in the reeds and there were bulldogs as well. If you were slow in walking the dogs would bite you. Thank god, my sister was so young and my mother was scared that she was going to cry. Nevertheless, fortunately, she never did, she was asleep, we sailed through the reeds, and we waited for the rest of people to go, we started crawling out of the stream. We went home and my mother gave us a cold bath and bathed herself as well, she couldn't warm the water, she was scared that maybe they might be other policemen who had remained still searching they would come, beat her up, since there was no human respect. She threw away all our clothes that we were wearing.

Talk of cuts and bruises; no one could talk about them besides just treat them quietly. It was as long as they are not life threatening. What did not treat the demonstration wounds salt, vinegar, barks of trees? She put us to sleep under the bed, because if the police officers were to come back they would pep through the windows see us on the bed. We slept under the bed, during that period the beds, which were there were steel springs and mattresses, not bases and mattresses that we have nowadays. My mother is my hero; I love my mum she means the world to me.

One thing that I remember mostly was the anger that children were exposed to, seeing their parents being humiliated and beaten, begging for mercy, the fact being this person is fighting for their human rights. Mostly, I think that is what made most of the young generation of blacks to go to war fight for freedom. That made children to hate white people. When I think of it, up to this day, these past political, discrimination situations that happened forty years ago still bring tears to my eyes. Some people survived the beatings, some were maimed for life, the so unlucky perished. It was clearly stated that people had to, abide by my government rules, or keep quiet, or else you die that was the Rhodesian government law for blacks.

The following day when my father returned home with my sister and brothers, he was very happy to see us all well and praised my mother; he said he knew she was going to make it. As we sat on my father's lap, together with my sister, I could see the happiness in my father's eyes. That was the life in the African townships up and down, whilst we had a rest we, could hear that there was no rest in other township. We lived up to it, but it was hard.

Chapter 2

I grew up fearing the white people because there was no relationship between the black Africans, and white Rhodesians. The attitude of white people towards blacks was very bad. The racism was not hidden at all, you could easily see it if you visit a white area only place. They use to call us kerfs Blacks, blacks never used the front door; they used back door. When I started going to school, started understanding English, I remember walking in town reading some of the notices, in black and white, "No black people allowed in this shop" that limited blacks from getting into some shops. Whites had their own bus stops, their bus drivers were white as well, we had our own black bus drivers, bus stops, and we had our own toilets. which had a permanent stench emanating form, which could be smelt from a distance. Even by the town centre there were areas designated for blacks where by the outskirts of the town Salisbury (now Harare). I remember each time we were going shopping, my mother would ask us to go to use the toilet before we leave home. I grew up thinking that the whites never go to the toilet the way we did, because of the superiority complex they showed us.

However, that never stopped us venturing into finding out why we were treated differently the anger grew inside as we grew older into adults. When I was much younger I never understood, why in our townships we lived had time restrictions, which restricted us from moving late at night. When our relatives visit us, my parents had to take them to the police station in our township. At the police station, visitors were given an authorisation note with stipulated days allowed to visit. Because when the police patrol officers, do a random check they would ask for the household registration card. In case of an additional head they would request a note of authorisation to stay number of days requested. In case of time elapse, you needed to renew it on the day of expiry. It was tough and rough.

That led to imaging of black African leaders to start organising the recognition of the black people in the townships and mostly the martial laws and restrictions of movement. I remember the police reserves dressed in naïve blue uniforms, which use to patrol in our townships at night, to check on what was going on at night, I think they knew that there were meetings going on. Black people were very clever they use to have their meetings in darkness, plan all their strategies for the next demonstrations where to take place what time.

They practiced certain whistling that signals that their fellow black men would interpret easily, whilst having meetings. Some of the whistling was an all clear informing. Others were alerting danger coming so that they could switch off the light if they had light up a candle, to be quiet, other alerted to no movement at all. Stay put hide. The signal person was the most trusted person of all the people carrying out a meeting because if he fails to communicate with the next person, there would be some casualties. In other cases the whistling communicator, would misled the police reserve to misguide them to a different place all together so that others would quickly move from the danger area. It uses to be two or more good whistlers.

They had a way of communicating although there were no messaging systems that have come into play these days. I remember whistling was banned; if caught, whistling one could be arrested or beaten by the police, due to the fact that they suspected them as the night whistlers. This also made some of my nephews to be very vulnerable, as they liked whistling at night just to provoke the police.

Times were changing as I was growing up because black people realized that they were not free in their own motherland. There were loads of strikes and demonstrations and guerrilla warfare, the Rhodesian government realised that there was no going back for these blacks.

Bombs were exploding right in the town centre. The one that shocked the whole country was the bomb, which landed on the shell BP, in Salisbury, (now Harare). I remember that we could see the fire from as far as other townships, which were situated fifteen to twenty kilometres away. It rained for more than a week.

The Rhodesian government adjusted a number of its discriminatory laws. Things started changing as the law started to be lenient blacks were in a position to go in the same buses as their fellow citizens white Rhodesians. They were areas, designated for whites only, and blacks now had the right to go there. The Rhodesian government decided to have a meeting with the blacks of Rhodesia, in order to stop the war, and have a code of understanding.

The Rhodesian government requested all the African opposition parties to participate in the parliament elections, which were coming on that year. The black freedom fighters did not participate in those elections. To the government surprise, the freedom fighters party never participated. Nothing changed there was still a war after the parliament elections. Because black people of Zimbabwe were not concerned. What one of these opposition parties managed to bring was recognition of black teacher's better pay.

The fact still remains that, we had our own buses, bus stations, designated towards our townships, black townships, designated nearer the industrial areas, and our own shops, parks and entertainment centres. Black people of then Rhodesia learned to live their lives in their own townships, built, in the midst of air-polluted areas, recycled water and people survived by the grace of god. My mother use to boil the water again, or else we would all suffer with diarrhoea the whole family and it was not a good sight since we had one toilet. Therefore, we grew up not drink water straight from the tape.

The first township built was then Harare, in this township people use to walk in the street day in day out. Even the police feared going into that township, due to people revolting towards police. It consisted of people of all occupations, but mostly, people who were working in the industrial area since this township were built amongst the industrial areas. In big cities like Harare (then Salisbury), industries were springing up so labour was needed.

At first, the white people did not want to build houses for blacks even though they needed them to do all the hard work. They decided to build hostels where only men allowed living. These hostels were built within walking distance from the industrial sites. Their families had to stay back in the rural areas or Tribal Trust Lands (T.T.L's) as they called them. These hostels were blocks of flats with single rooms, communal kitchens, bathrooms and toilets. Each room would house several men and wives were not allowed to visit their husbands.

Still some men used to smuggle their wives and girlfriend into the hostels but if they were caught they would be arrested, had to pay a fine then put on the buses back to their rural homes. Some would end up on the streets where they would be arrested again. It was a tough life for the black majority. Most men had to visit their families back in the rural areas on weekends or at the end of the month when they were paid. These hostels were becoming more and more overcrowded. Hygiene became a big problem because of many people sharing few bathrooms and toilets. There was also a permanent stench emanating from these hostels, which could be smelt from a distance.

Because of the expanding industries and the need for more labour, the government realised they had to provide more housing for workers and their families. They built houses around the industrial areas. This is when townships (for black people), as they were called then, sprung up. These were Harare National (now called Mbare), Highfield, where I grew up, Mabvuku, Tafara, Mufakose, Kambuzuma. These townships were strategically built in order for the industrialists to obtain cheap labour. They never considered that the pollution by smoke and the noise coming from the industries would be harmful to people's health. Besides every township there was police camps strategically build to control black people's movement. Other black nationalities of Rhodesia by then were not interested in joining the police force or army.

Firstly, it was mostly people from (Fort Victoria) now Masvingo who were going for policing jobs and security guards, which other Rhodesian black nationals considered, that it was for people who had no remorse. Black people hated them and use to call them, names, e.g. (BSAP) British South African Police, were called, *Broke Soon After Pay*. On the other hand security guards were, chanted at, "*if they beat you up, beat them back they are not police men*", do not be afraid. Usually they use to work at night guarding building or sit on the door of a shop. Passersby would chant at them, like those who use to sit with a guarding dog, calling them, unspeakable names, some would ask how's your wife, meaning the guard dog. These guards would not do anything besides to just keep quiet, because that was provocation and if they chase after street passerby's you lose your job. Police officers were able to use the public transport free and they use to stand on the standing areas in the bus.

Chapter 3
Freedom of movement, migration for the black Africans

The Declaration of the Federation (1953), for the migration of black people from Northern Rhodesia, Nyasaland were specifically meant to provide labour to the white farmers, industry al sector, the mining sector of the country, of the Southern Rhodesia. By the look of it, Rhodesia had a high potential of the production of agricultural produce and mining of minerals, which had a high turnover on the international market. That boosted the Rhodesian economy, which was benefiting only the white people. In any case, mobility migration of black people within this region was immense due to black people being poor in their countries of origin, and looking for greener pastures. My grandfather was originally from Malawi. It also introduced intermarriages, because most of the migrant workers were young when they migrated from their countries.

Most of the people working in towns were foreign migrant workers. Besides the industrialists, the other employer was the local council, which was responsible for providing sanitation to city dwellers. The sewage system was nonexistent in the townships and workers were responsible for collecting buckets full of excrement and garbage.

The foreign workers covered the economic sector that most local people never wanted to work in. foreigners were also employed foreigners as domestic workers by most white families who provided them with accommodation in the back yard. These little houses were called 'boy's' kaya and they were meant to be for single people. Most of them had no electricity. No visitors were allowed. When these workers were off duty they used to sit outside their bosses' gates, where they would meet other workers and socialise. If they had visitors, they would meet along the roadside, somewhere. It was indeed a tough life!

At first, all blacks were paid cash in hand by their employers. Blacks did not have bank accounts. As time went by the whites discovered that they were missing a lucrative business so they introduced a building society for blacks called the central African Building Society. My father was one of the first people to open a savings account at this bank.

My mother use to save my father's wages in any old tin of biscuits. My father bought a two bed roomed house in Highfield and we moved in from the rural areas with him. These houses consisted of just the shell; it had no window glasses, no flooring and no doors inside. One had to buy and finish off all the other finishing's. On windows, people use to improvise and cover with plastic until they can afford to buy the glasses. As for floors, they had to put cement and the sand and look for a plaster to do the floors and inside walls, which were not plastered as well. We were quite comfortable in our little house but as the family expanded, the house was becoming too small. My father's wages were also becoming too little to support us all.

Workers fought for the right to stay in their houses even if they lost their jobs and the white government had to give in. these were mostly Malawian migrant workers like my father who had no rural homes. This resulted in most houses in townships owned by Malawians not by the local people. Workers also fought to be provided with larger houses for their growing families and the government allowed the local council to build more houses in the new townships of Glen Norah, Chitungwiza and Glen View. The local council also allowed black people who already had houses to extend them. There was no electricity in our houses and there were no street light. People use to get home as early as they can before dark. We had a life, although not good enough. It was full of intimidation and laws were hard to abide, because of the inconsistence. Laws were changed following the situation in the African townships.

The Rhodesian government introduced of building society savings banks and commercial banks to black Africans. Black Africans started receiving their wages through the banks and the post office. The post office was mostly used for sending money telegrams for those who were immigrants and had come to Rhodesia to work, especially Malawians and Zambians. It came as a surprise, since this option of money laundering was for whites and coloured people only. Because of the realisation that they were losing out bank charges and mortgage interests by not offering options of mortgages and money launderings to the black people. This recognition of losing interest from the black majority people who were by now doing well in life. Most banks introduced mortgages, money launderings to all races. This offered mortgages at high interest.

For those who had managed to buy their own houses, they offered building loans for extensions and rebuilding. It was very attractive, black people did go for it, some are still paying because it was a long term, minimum was ten years and maximum twenty five years. I remember that my father refused he preferred to buy bits and pieces until he sees that he is in a position to start rebuilding our house. The mortgage interests were high. However, with the help of my mother selling vegetables, father working as a driver, our house was build within a year. I remember coming home to a new house which we all had a bedroom and a kitchen within the same roof. It was exciting and a joy to be in your own room, and after being naught to be send to your own room, which was a joy rather than a misery. We all had a bed, a wardrobe, and a dressing table.

As far as the realisation of black Africans majority rule was concerned, it had to be because black people in the Tribal Trust Lands were tired of being beaten and exposed to danger most of the time and the way they were living, and for those with relatives working in the former government army, were either killed or maimed. People's private parts were mutilated, e.g. lips, ears were cut off if they suspected that you were a sell-out to the government, which was ruling at that time.

Historically Rhodesia was more properly the British colony of Southern Rhodesia was founded upon an institutionalised form of discrimination not unlike the apartheid system in neighbouring South Africa. Blacks, who made up the overwhelming majority of the population, were excluded from political power and were only allowed to farmland in designated areas. At independence, the rural areas were divided almost equally between European and African land 18-million hectares apiece. Yet there were roughly one hundred times as many African farmers as whites and African-designated land was almost exclusively in the regions with poorer soil and rainfall.

It was very easy for the black Africans of Rhodesia to mobilize to fight a war against oppression of the white minority of Rhodesia. This was exacerbated by the anger that the young generations of the black majority of Zimbabwe had against the white people, due to the exposure of the beatings and humiliation. Black people of Rhodesia wanted to revenge and wanted their country back to them. Mostly, it was due to the anguish, which caused the township raids th   became Prime Minister but real power still rested with the white-controlled state structures. In late 1979, all parties attended a conference sponsored by Britain, the nominal colonial power, at Lancaster House in London.

A constitution and formula for the transition to independence was agreed. In elections in March 1980, Mugabe's ZANU-PF gained an absolute majority of seats in Parliament, with ZAPU taking most of the remainder, apart from 20 per cent of seats reserved for the white electorate under the Lancaster House constitution. Zimbabwe became independent in April 1980 with Robert Mugabe as Prime Minister at the head of a coalition government largely composed of ZANU-PF and ZAPU. The new government embarked on an important series of reforms to extend social benefits such as health care and universal primary education to the whole population. Many of the worst human rights criminals fled the country at independence, often to find similar positions within the South African security apparatus.

An attempt to challenge the status quo by non-violent political methods was met with repression. In the early 1960s ZAPU AND ZANU were banned and their leaders, detained without trial. In November 1965 the Rhodesian, government declared a State of Emergency, which gave it powers, many for years at a time. On November 11, 1965, a few days after introducing the state of emergency, the Rhodesian Front government led by Ian Douglas Smith, made a Unilateral Declaration of Independence from Britain, which signalled an increase in the repression of Black Nationalism and an end to any hope of peaceful

Constitutional reform, in the late 1960s the nationalist parties launched an armed struggle against the (technically illegal) Rhodesian regime, which from 1972 onwards developed into major bush war. The regime used increased brutal methods to suppress nationalist agitation. The scope of the death penalty was dramatically extended and there were dozens of secret executions of opponents. Torture was systematic and widespread, and included beatings, electric shocks and immersion in water until the victim lost consciousness. ***The introduction of the Selous Scouts in the Matabeleland area by the Rhodesian government was to increase intimidation to the rural people, in the sense that they recruited black Africans to join them and pretend that everything was well and there was no war going on. Others were more of civilians (black Zimbabweans), wearing their day clothes and were used to secretly investigate about the whereabouts of the freedoms fighters.***

The security forces responded to the bush was by indiscriminate measures against the rural population. Three quarters of a million rural Zimbabweans were moved into protected villages. The idea, which originated with the British in Malaya, practiced by the United States in Vietnam, and has been followed by several other governments in devising counter insurgent strategies, was to isolate the civilian population from the guerrillas by forcing them to live in compounds. Villagers were forced to stay in the protected villages by strict dusk to dawn curfews. Curfew breakers were shot. Forced removals combined with the curfew meant that some could not reach their fields to cultivate. In the first year of protected villages in one area, deaths increased by 37 per cent. Eighty per cent of these were from starvation and one in every five adults (let alone children, who were more vulnerable) suffered from malnutrition. Parallel with the protected villages' policy was "Operation Turkey," the army's ironic name for a policy of destroying food supplies in the rural areas. The ostensible aim was to allow only the barest minimum of food to reach the rural population so that they would have none to share with the guerrillas. The Rhodesian army burned down kraals and granaries, closed shops and grinding mills and shot cattle. The combined effect of the protected villages and Operation Turkey was to increase the demoralization and war weariness of the people and arguably, to create pressure on the leaders of the nationalist parties to accept less favourable terms for independence than they might otherwise have held out for. At independence, the outlying areas of Zimbabwe faced an acute food crisis as a direct result of these policies.

The realisation of failing to control the black people of Rhodesia to fight against the Rhodesian forces led them to the introduction of call-up of black people secondary qualified students after finishing their secondary school. They were trained in artillery, air forces. They were deployed to fight against their fellow brothers in the bush fighting for the liberation of the black majority rule. It was very unsuccessful. It failed to materialise due to the realisation of whom they were fighting and for what reason. For those who voluntarily joined the Rhodesian forces and were married they had very attractive incentives. The families were well looked after whilst their husbands were in the bush fighting the war. It did not go on for a long time until they had to let go the young men who did not go to join the forces voluntarily.

However, most of those who were permanently employed as the Rhodesian forces stayed on; there were many of the Rhodesian forces who were also killed during this war.

*   Richard Carver and David Sanders, "Why Soames will have to speed food to war zones,"
     Sunday Times, London, December 23 1979.

Chapter 4

Now let me introduce you to my life revelations. I have always been a woman of adventure always willing to learn. How we came up to be selling vegetables was due to my mother, who realised that my father's wages were not enough to fully support the family, although it was more of an embarrassment to my father, because people, (the society) were seeing him as incapable of not being able to look after his family. My mother was against women oppression. My father resorted to buying everything needed in the house. My mother kept on looking for money to start her vegetable business. She got 50 shillings from one of my father's nephew, which she bought a pocket of oranges, sold them out on the roadside, to passer-bys from the football stadium Harare, Zimbabwe. She made a bit of profit. She insisted on carrying on with her business although my father was a bit apprehensive, since my father was a man who understood and realised that, what my mother was doing was helping the family to meet its financial needs. My father still provided with money for groceries every weekend to buy the basic commodities, e.g. meat and grounded maize meal, bathing soap and marmalade jam his favourite, for his sandwiches, as a child I hated marmalade jam, but now it is one of my favourite.

My mother soon realised the need to expand her business and she joined a local women's club, which was been formed by other women who were business minded, and wanted to better themselves their families' lives and against women oppression. They knew that they needed to work very hard in order to raise their families' financial status. They also taught women sewing, cookery, housekeeping, dressing competitions, childcare, and first aid.

They also started going back to school; they attended night schools because amongst these women, some of them could not read, neither write. However, amazingly they knew how to count money and calculate their profit. They started reading, writing, buying the newspaper (Herald) reading the current news, those who were good at English would translate to their fellow women and discuss. I use to enjoy hearing my mother discussing the current affairs with my father. My father was educated, more than my mother, but my mother was very intelligent when it comes to being organised, I can say she could multi task things. As their ventures expanded, the women realised that they needed some remises to do their business.

Within the society if there was anything that, they did not agree with they would demonstrate peacefully, their grievances were solved because since the Rhodesian government realised that the majority of the black society consisted of women. They demonstrated for anything that was political incorrectness and they usually were replied, by having a meeting with the government officials. They fought for time restrictions for the movement of people at night to be removed and the Rhodesian government met it. They decided to approach their Local Council to give them land and assist them in building markets near all the local Shopping Centres in every black community township.

They started going around other black townships to mobilise and encourage other women to join in and carry out the vegetable markets for the well-being of their families and the liberalisation of women to be allowed to work. These were very busy shopping centres, especially over the weekends, which was accessible to many black people from other townships or from rural areas. Firstly, the council built some temporary shelters and asked the women to provide their own tables on which to display their vegetables and traditional wares, such as clay pots, wooden spoons, and handmade doormats, summer sunhats, tie-and-dye materials, snuffs and other traditional goods.

As time goes by, on which the council decided to build a proper and more secure market building with stand numbers and also water taps were put nearby within the market, lock up under the stand storage. These were allocated to the women and those who joined in later were put on waiting lists, and were allocated as others retire or move to other areas of their dwellings. They also built toilets, which were for the market people and their customers.

There was an allocated Council cleaner to look after the surrounding areas of the market. The council registered all the traders and asked them to pay weekly rentals. They also decided to expand the whole shopping complex and offered land to black people on which to build more shops. Black people built convenient stores, service stations, hairdressers' shops, chemists and hardware shops. Amongst these businesses built by emerging African businesspersons and women was a little barber's shop. Mr Joshua Nkomo himself used to go and have his hair cut in this little shop quite regularly. I personally met him there as a young girl and am still very proud to have known him.

Open-air music by emerging African musicians was held every Saturday afternoon at an open space near the market. The township grew very fast. Moreover, we could see other tourists from Europe visiting our shops to buy souvenirs to take back home, caved stones, walking sticks, snuff, flower pots made out of wood, and clay, tie and dye materials and tee shirts.

As for Africans Sunday's were always for worshipping, every family use to go to church and most of the families also created social centres through the church gatherings. It was a society that almost had it all, besides all the hardships of segregation and discrimination. I witnessed the first fish and chip shop at Machipisa, which was opened by an African family. Before this, we had never eaten fish and chips! We used to either roast our potatoes on an open fire or just boil them. It was as if a McDonald's shop opened for the first time in a remote African village! My eldest sister got a job in the fish and chip shop as a cashier. I used to wait for her when she finished work so I could share the leftover fish and chips that her manager gave her.

My mother was a very serious businesswomen and she showed us how she was making some profit from her fruit and vegetable sales. She used to order her vegetables from a wholesale market at the main Harare market (now called Mbare). She used to teach us some marketing techniques how to present the fruit and vegetables to attract customers and customer care in general. Her policy was never argued with customers, as the customer was always right. I learnt that a seller's aim should be to sell their goods as fast as possible so as make a profit and to sell the produce while it is still fresh. When customers were satisfied, they will always come back for more. My mother also used to offer credit to some of her customers after gaining trust in them. They in turn would introduce more customers to her.

The council used to carry out unannounced inspections at the market stalls so it was very important to maintain high standards of hygiene and cleanliness. Inspectors would also check the fruits and vegetables for freshness. These were carried out to ensure that customers were buying uncontaminated food.

My mother and her colleagues who operated in the fruit and vegetable market business were very hard working and most of these women managed to afford to pay for their children's education. Most children of these women went on to pursue successful careers in many fields; for example, some became doctors, nurses, lawyers, accountants, bankers, teachers and other professions. Some managed to pay their children to go and study overseas in countries like Britain and America. Some women managed to help their husbands extend their houses and paid electricity to be installed in their houses. Some managed to buy electrical gadgets like fridges, stoves, televisions big stereos that were considered luxuries in those days. Some people in the area where I lived used to throw parties at Christmas as a way of showing off their wealth and they would invite all the neighbours. They would provide food and drinks. They would dress their children in expensive clothes for all to see. Just as well, the women also took to the trend of moving with time, in fashion, and in weekend pastimes like going to the horse race courses. Borrowdale was the place to be, besides having black designated areas. They did bet as a syndicate or as individuals.

By then our father was in a position to afford to support extended family members who would come and stay with us every now and then. In the African culture families are very closely knit and it is considered as an insult to ask a visiting relative how long they are going to stay. My brothers, sisters and I had to put up with sleeping on the floor at times in order to accommodate respected visiting elderly relatives.

By then, my father had changed his attitude about my mother carrying out her business and had become supportive. My brothers, sisters, and I used to help our mother at the market after school and on weekends. At first, we thought our parents were abusing us by making us work so hard but now I think this hard work has paid off as it gave us a good foundation for our lives. It has taught me that when one is climbing up a ladder, one needs to remember every step that one takes so that when you fall you can hold on to one of the steps, pick yourself up and then carry on from there. I am sure you can see where I am coming from. I learnt to work hard from a very early age and it is now paying off.

Most of our mother's use to go home around five in the afternoon and left us to sell the left over produce. Equipped with the knowledge that we had learned from our mothers, we would try to sell the vegetable so that when we go home with a lot of money our mother will be very grateful and that means a lot of pocket money. We use to call customers and tell them that we have a lot to offer and other products are now free.

One evening I mistook one man who was already buying from our neighbours, stall for my uncle, the man quickly apologised came to us. He bought most of our left over vegetables. My sister and I had to help him carry, what he had bought to his car. My sister did not say anything, she could not look me into the eyes, because the other woman was so furious and standing akimbo, and just watching. We finished parking our goods and we ran home. Moreover, as soon as we opened the gate we busted into laughter that my mother was thinking we had run away from the police officer, because maybe we did not close the store in time.

The store use to be closed at 19:00hrs, and if you extend the time you would be arrested and pay a fine. Sometimes, as children we would run away if they ask us to go with them to the police station. We asked our mother to count the money we had, and she wondered how we had so much, we told her what had happened and the whole family laughed.

The following day this lady the owner of the next stall told my mother what had happened, my mother apologised and said that is the way kids behave that is why most of go home and leave them. In a way, she was trying to tell her to leave her children and let them enjoy the stall and the experience. She uses to be on her shop from morning until closing down time. Each time we think of that incident with my sister especially, we still laugh, and all I can say is, "Oh! Gone are the days when we enjoyed life in Rhodesia".

We use to enjoy going to assist mother at the vegetable shop, because mom uses to spoil us with money to the hairdresser's and to the musical festivals were occasionally held in the football stadiums. We have seen them all, those musicians who visited our country, like the Percy Sledge, The Hurricanes, Miriam Makeba, Ladysmith Black mambazo, from South Africa, and other famous Zimbabwean musician, like Thomas Mapfumo, Oliver Mtukudzi. Life was just good for us; we use to go shopping with my father for our clothes and school uniforms. We had a very strong bond amongst our parents and ourselves.

These market place vegetable salespersons broke the chain of freedom of women, "some call it women liberalisation," they were allowed to work, participate in politics and in any society problems they were living in. They became the voice of black women. During that time, we had enough money to live on. These women managed to help their husbands to buy the title deeds for their houses, helped extended their houses to give a good comfort to their families. We saw the introduction of electricity in their houses. Telephone lines were there for their communication purposes with their sons and daughters now staying away from home, or have travelled to study in Europe. Talk of televisions and Supersonic radios, it was now more of a competition than a luxury, as to what do you have in your household? The luxury started to flow. Electrical appliances were now a necessity for the home.

Houses became homes, very coarse. We were never disadvantaged as such, we went to school, fees were paid and we use to enjoy all the family talks and jokes that our father uses to share with us. Christmas parties were more of a show of rather than a celebration, because of the food that was put on the table and the guests who use to be invited, and the kids were dressed in those expensive designer clothes. Although sometimes we use to think, it was child abuse. We started working at a very early age, working for our little lives. But I assume it has rewarded us, in the sense that we learned that when climbing a ladder you need to remember every step that you take, so that when you fall you can hold on to one of the steps then you can pick yourself up then go on from there.

As the townships were now growing into small towns and becoming popular, we saw the building of proper recreation centres, football stadiums started cropping up as well. Bandits, especially criminals, who would be saving their crimes committed in the society, were sentenced to work in the development of the townships. They built sewage pipes, built the football stadiums which where situated in the nearby townships. Nearer every football stadium, there was also built a council beer garden, which sold the African beer brew. The English beer, which was sold in a pub upstairs for those who were earning more wages and could afford to buy expensive English beer. The set up of having a bus station, a stadium and a beer garden situated at the same proximity use to annoy many housewives, because their husbands would just get there and spend all their pay check before they get home on every Friday. Some housewives use to stand by the bus stop to get some monies out of their husbands before it is all spend. It was such an interesting sight, to see.

Some of the situations were quite embarrassing and others were more of dramatic when the wives snatch off the pay envelopes from their husbands. We had it all; it was a society, which was full of humour and serious business sometimes.

Chapter 5

As you can now imagine were the observer is coming from, started observing from afar at a very early age. It is fortunate that she learned the knit gritty of life at an early age. As far as school was concerned according to the Rhodesian Government, we had to go to school because it was necessary for each parent to send their off springs to school and pay school fees. That was one good thing about the Rhodesian Government. We learnt a lot more than children of nowadays. The teachers were very dedicated to give the right education. They had the respect from the society and they had decent salaries. The thing is you had to be educated to get somewhere in life, and surely you would reap the fruits of your labour. We all did go to school in my family, and some of us we still had a lot at the back of our minds.

Firstly, I worked at the old age home to raise money to study. Moreover, that was my first experience at the age of sixteen years that is when I came across emptying commodes at that tender age. In addition, from previous rumours as a child we use to wonder whether whites go to the toilet. We never thought that they did. Due the superiority, they had in the society as first class citizens of Rhodesia. After a year my father removed me from that job, he was not very happy to hear about what the job entailed. Then I came back home and got a job to work as a shop assistant. That one I worked for some time, and I was maturing and trying for other jobs.

I did go to the public service offices that recruited government staff. I was given a form and asked to fill it and come the following day for an interview. I did not sleep with the excitement and I even failed to eat dinner, I had butterflies in my stomach. Because these jobs where firstly for whites and coloured people only, but the doors had opened for us now that we had the qualifications to join the civil service. I attended my interview at ten o'clock the following day. I felt a bit low and had no hope because they were many of us, and we wrote a test in English and a bit of mathematics.

After the test, we were seated in the waiting room. They urgently needed staff, by the look of it. Therefore, we were given our test results told who got the job after two hours. We had drinks tea, coffee and soft drinks, but nobody touched it, it was nerve racking. When the door opened, the interviewers came in with a list, and told us that if your name is not called try again next time. When my name was called, I was numb from head to toe. I only managed to say thank you and was told which ministry I was going to, and I was asked to report for duty on a Monday. I got home my mother asked me how it was, I could not talk, she asked me if I wanted something to eat, I managed to just say no! I went to bed and cried my eyes out with disbelief. Because this was an out of reach job, during those days.

I spend the whole day in my room until when my father came from work and asked how I was, my mother said she didn't know, my father called me he thought I didn't get the job, I started crying, and he comforted me reassured that I should try next time, since you were given an opportunity to try again. I told my father that I got the job, to his disbelief, he shed some tears with joy, and asked me why I was upset, I told him that, this was the least expectation that I expected to happen to me in my life. He offered me some money to go and buy good clothes for an office job. My eldest brothers gave me money too to buy myself underclothes as he stated it. That weekend was full of joy, happiness, and celebration.

I started working as a registry clerk; it was very interesting to find that it was a mixture of all colours of people. Moreover, the head of the registry was an Indian woman very nice and she is the one who carried out the training for new recruits, and all the in-house training for registry clerks. In addition, after a week I found myself offered my own desk and my codex that I used for filing letters in alphabetic order. I enjoyed going to work every day and the fact that now I was able now to wake up in the morning and catch a bus to work. The fact of just being in the city centre and working in the city centre made someone to be class and trend. I started following my passion for fashion. I dressed well, and followed every trend that was there during those days. Platform shoes, bellbottoms, afro wigs, knee-high stockings I did wore them all. The time stilettos were in fashion we were there, still following the fashion. I joining the modelling agency, I tried my luck, but my height let me down.

As time progressed, the banks started recruiting blacks as bank tellers and clerks. I was on the move again. I started with the building society because the commercial banks had not opened up yet. I join the Central African Building Society. The salary was good and now all the luxuries that I wanted were now there. I worked as a clerk in the client's queries department. I use to update clients' passbook as they were called those days, enter their interest if it was not entered in their passbooks, and update their accounts in the codex.

After a few years, I decided to move on because acquired enough experience to join the commercial banks. I got a job as a relief bank teller that meant that, needed cover anywhere in the country where we had a branch, I would go for as long as I was needed there. Some of the covering lasted up to three weeks or more. That made me travel and adventure the country's big and small towns. I had an out of town allowance and I stayed in the five star hotels with full meals. I had the time of my life.

After a few years working in the bank, my father was now retired and my mother was now retired as well. My eldest sister, took over mother's vegetable market place, she was also

doing very well as a single mother of two. Both my elder brothers were doing very well, one as a sales representative and the other one was working in the purchasing and supplying office by the industrial area. We all assisted looking after our parents. We had a certain standard that we maintained in our family. This is more like a trademark. Four o'clock tea every relative of ours knows about that, and eight o'clock supper. I continued with my work at the bank and the war was going on.

Besides all the fear and intimidation that the Rhodesian government instilled in black people's minds, still people did took a lot of risk. Well history explains itself, that these people organized and mobilized a bush war that was against the oppression of the white rule of our country. As time moved on there were other people who were growing up started to see the problems of whites ruling the country for that matter, they were the minority of the society had more rights than the black majority.

Most of the European countries started offering training for the freedom fighters. Whereby young people who went to go to fight the war went, settled, and came to fight from the bases. There was an outcry sometimes when we use to here that the camps were bombed by the Rhodesian regime, and a number of youngsters perished. It was hard to think of it, because youngsters use to run away from home without telling their fathers and mothers that we are going to the war. Bless them, for what they did for the sake of freedom.

Well this did not take a long time for the black majority of people to realize that this is our country and why should we be treated like guests in our motherland. One thing that people of Zimbabwe learned was to study hard and get to be educated and compete with the white minority. Black people of Zimbabwe demonstrated this by starting to qualify for those posts that were not meant for them. The government had no choice but to just give them the job with a low wage.

On the other hand, one does not have to be negative about the Rhodesian government. There was a lot that was introduced to the black society of Rhodesia. We had organised transportation, the famous united buses! There had a timetable, and we all knew as and when one can get a bus to and from the town centre, Salisbury. Life was more organised, and black people use to reap fruits of their labour. For those who had qualification or training of some sort in their trading fields, they use to earn higher than those who were not educated. We also started seeing blacks joining the apprenticeship courses, fitter and turners, boilermakers, machine operators, etc. some went to the polytechnic college to do various courses, like, dressmaking, hairdressing, business studies, computer studies, electronic engineering, arts and craft, media communication and television presenting, mechanical engineering, architectural drawing and many more.

The Rhodesian government was now in a position to recognise the black population in some other challenging positions in the industry and commerce sector. Although for order white Rhodesians it was unbearable, they did not want to offer blacks the jobs..

Life during Zimbabwean Period

Chapter 6
Independence and the political crisis

Getting our independence, in 1980 was every Zimbabwean's dream that came true; I always wonder was it a genuine thing for us blacks to get our independence or it was a mockery?

* The sense of hope and optimism that accompanied the birth of Zimbabwe as an independent state in 1980 survived for several years. In keeping with his promises about reconciliation, Robert Mugabe strove to build a good working relationship with his former white adversaries. He appointed two white ministers to his cabinet and retained the services of the former Rhodesian armed forces commander, General Peter Walls, as the country's military chief. He even kept in place the head of intelligence, Ken Flower, who had previously spent considerable effort trying to organise Mugabe's assassination. At one of their first meetings in Mugabe's office, Flower was anxious to explain about the various attempts that the Rhodesians had made to kill him.* because, *Regardless of their crimes, the Rhodesian officials had to stay, because of the well-being of the security apparatus depended on it. The other reason for extending an olive branch to Rhodesian security officials was political. Mugabe was eager to avoid antagonizing the economically crucial white community. Although many whites migrated soon after independence, the farming community has generally stayed and benefited from an agricultural boom, whilst whites occupied many important positions in commerce and business. All ministers and government and government servants were indemnified under Rhodesian law for acts carried out in good faith in defence of national security. However, there was no indication that the Zimbabwean government ever considered the possibility of nullifying the indemnity legislation in order to prosecute the human rights violators. In these circumstances, the Zimbabwean government decided that reconciliation rather than prosecution best served the interests of national stability.

* The state of Africa, *"A decree of violence"*

* Quoted in Bill Berkeley, One Party Fits all," *The New Republic*, March 6, 1989.

* Berkeley comments: "Some Zimbabweans cite that record as precedent for sweeping the more recent conflict under the rug."

The old system was running in parallel with the old system that is in the security of the country but the thing is it was not known that we were still having the Rhodesian government security adopted system through and through. The implementation of the new systems to meet the people of Zimbabwe's needs security wise was never met. There still was a lot of intimidation in the air. Anyone who was in the Zimbabwean forces, be it a soldier, or policeman they still were harassing people or even killing people without being sentenced, properly, justice was never met for the people of Zimbabwe.

Sheepishly, we never understood what was in store for us. The fact remains that the country, (Zimbabwe) failed economically and politically. Politics become difficult to understand, when you try to figure out what went wrong. Well, we had support; we were offered to study abroad with all the financial support. After the war, many options for black young Zimbabwean to advance in their careers were offered to study within or abroad. Some of us managed to strike a chance to study abroad, under the United Nations programme, to assist the development of the country and the economy growth. I was very excited to apply for the scholarships, which were offered then. Therefore, I tried my luck and got the scholarship to go and study, and I managed to keep the secret to myself. I only told my parents when I had the air-ticket in my hand. They did throw a good party for me, and gave their blessing. I left home, and went to study abroad.

I did left home, to go and study, and that was the important thing in my mind to study. These studying programmes set up by the Zimbabwean government on a short team programme to enable Zimbabwean blacks to study in the fields that needed developing and to occupy the jobs that had no black people in them. We did travel well and when we arrived at the destination of the country, we went to study, and the first thing we felt the cold weather. It was cold and freezing. We were allocated to a student hostel, where we met other students from other countries as well. I remember we were in thousands. So we were distributed according to our areas of specialisation. Finally, we all went our separate ways. We stayed in that hostel for two days to a week depending on the distance you were going. We had a guide who spoke English then, and she would advise us and arrange our air or train tickets. Then she will see that we got in the right train, and advise the train attendant to drop us at the right station, and in a case where there is already other Zimbabwean, they would let them know that there are other country people coming and can you come, meet them, and help them settle.

We arrived late, and it was already snowing and we were really frozen. They came two people from Zimbabwe and they introduced themselves to us. Them the other university guide took us with them to the new student's hostel, where we were given a mattress sheets blankets and pillows. Most of us, lost our luggage, and the clothes that we had were the ones we were wearing and we use to wash our under garments at night then wear them in the morning, thank god there were heating systems. We use to dry our clothes there. The following day we were called, and asked to go to the dean for foreign students, and were we had our students Identification cards done and we went to the cash office to get our first stipend. We got our pocket money for food. Then from there we were taken to the shop by one of the foreign student office buyer, I suppose, we went to a big shop which was full of winter things. She asked us if we could pick jackets, hats, scarves, stockings, boots, winter underwear and she advised us to pick over size, because as foreigners we tend to wear a lot underneath the jackets. The way we were happy to beat the cold out of us, it was an amazing feeling. I have never felt like that.

We studied hard our hope was to go back home and help develop our country. We use to read day in day out. The first year was very hard learning a new language and a new life style and new language. We were now able to communicate with our fellow students who were French, Spanish speakers. We now had a lot in common, we could have lunches or dinners together, and then soon after the language-learning year we did not travel out of the country because we were not allowed yet, because they feared that if we go away for two months we might forget the language. It was very helpful in a way. Otherwise, the university send us to a resting place for the summer holiday together with our language teachers. We had a nice time, but homesickness use to kick off, and we use to suffer from depression.

Even amongst students, those who were already there, especially from Matebeleland area in Zimbabwe had some reservation against those from Mashonaland due to the War that was still going on in Matebeleland. Eventually as students, also due to the integration of the two parties ZANU-PF and ZAPU there was a great feeling of togetherness. We were treated the same got pocket money from home Zimbabwe at the embassy together we could collect for others. We had to organise our own students meetings during holidays to air our views or just to socialise as people from the same country. We had good student relationships, and a sense of unity was formed.

After the first year at the university now, we had our first year examinations waited for the results, so that we could now travel wherever we wanted, but still there were excursions at the university if you wanted, or those who wanted to work, could go for construction. We use to have two months holidays every year, we learned to travel in Europe, and we even use to travel all over Europe including England. As students, we use to work in shops or cleaning in hotels.

Whilst on holiday I travelled to England worked at Kensington Palace hotel. It was by choice to work for extra money to shop around, since we had also pocket money from home. Towards the end of our holiday, we would travel slowly, back to the university. On the way, back we would visit Europe for two or a week like in Holland or Germany, and then proceed through other European countries then when we reach the borderline of our destination we would understand that we are back to university. We studied hard, finished our university, and graduated with flying colours. There were endless welcome parties, and the dream was there, not knowing what was in store for us. When we returned home, thinking it was according to the government plan. We were let down because the other member of the part, relative had already filled in the post. So, after struggling in Europe to achieve a Qualification to be able to help build country's economy, was a more of a joke.

One had to look for alternative solutions, to be recognized or get a job, because of the bureaucracy that had its machinery in place, they would make it a point that you are from the top brass in order for you to occupy that post. In any case, we survived. We managed to end up landing in teaching posts that were easy to get as long as you have a degree. This was now a different place, and ***our dreams were shattered***.

We learned that after trying very hard to get to the promised job. Some quickly got out of the country. Others we had all the faith in our country but we did walked out with our knowledge, which was meant for Zimbabwe.

My dreams were shattered, I use to go for walks, and I was very disillusioned. With my friend, whom I had the same qualifications with; we tried to go to the ministry that we were supposed to be working one of the ministry secretaries laughed at us and openly told us over his dead body we will get the jobs. I will never forget the grin he had on his face, each time he appeared on the television I use to switch it off, but actually I forgave him but I will never forget.

The fact that we were over qualified for the other posts, which were there, they would rather have people from the local colleges. I had a tough time, my father died when I was studying abroad; I never got the time to attend his funeral, in this process of looking for a job. I was grieving under those circumstances, I was very angry with the government. The fact that I did this to help the country just made me stay in bed the whole day I was very depressed. I always ask myself, why did I put myself through this, and for whom?

As an observer from afar, I do not look for elements that are combustible that will create a fire if you rub them together. I suppose I am interested in the social structure within a given society, and the set up of a multi cultural society. The world is changing and if you look at the margins, you will find minority groups who have to bear the stigmata of the majority groups. I could not have hoped for anything better. The main reason I felt compelled to continue in prose was that I found it easier to describe certain political situation due to being there whilst it happened and also as they involved me personally and all the people from the third world countries.

Life was going on for others, in Zimbabwe, whilst others were suffering the atrocities of war, which was still going on in Matebeleland. Through my reading and researching and the wanting to know more, about what really happened I have come up to understand that the human rights of people was violated so much that it will never be repaired. Many people disappeared and many people were killed for no apparent reason. The perpetrators where never brought forward to courts and be charged for the atrocities they caused to the people of Zimbabwe. When it comes to tribalism, Zimbabweans do not have hard feelings for one another.

There are quite a number of issues that were mentioned. Nevertheless, people as usual they talked amongst themselves and even grieved amongst themselves. There was never support from the government, the only people who were worried about the people's welfare were the council of churches of Zimbabwe and The Amnesty International, which was usually blast fumed by the government of Zimbabwe. The Amnesty International was never taken serious when they reported of human rights violation, especially on prisoners.

Chapter 7
Crisis in Matebeleland

Looking back at the Matebeland crisis, one comes to the understanding that the electoral support for ZANU-PF and ZAPU in the 1980 election largely followed ethnic lines. All ZAPU's 20 seats came from Matabeleland where the predominant ethnic group is the Ndebele, or from the ethnically mixed Midlands. ZUNU-PF won no seats in Matebeland and drew most of its support from the majority Shone speakers. The original split between ZANU and ZAPU in the 1960s had nothing with the Ndebele-Shona division, but a combination of political accident and conscious tribalism by some party leaders combined to make it a potent factor by the time of independence.

The conflict first blew up in the army. At independence, it was agreed to integrate the ZANLA and ZIPRA** guerrillas into a single national army along side with the former Rhodesian forces. If anything, the former guerrillas were probably less prone to party or ethnic sectarianism than some of their political leaders. However, there was a widespread perception that the fighters who had made the greatest sacrifices for Zimbabwe's independence were having the least share benefits. Such frustration erupted into fighting between former ZANLA and ZIPRA guerrillas encamped at Entumbane Township in Bulawayo awaiting integration. Initial fighting in November 1980 died down after a few days.

*   Lawyers Committee, *op cit*, p90-1

*   The Zimbabwe African National Liberation Army (ZANLA) was the military wing of ZANU; the Zimbabwe People's Liberation Army (ZIPRA) was its ZAPU counterpart.

A second outburst in February 1981 spread to other groups of guerrillas awaiting integration and was only ended when the government deployed ex-Rhodesians units and their air force against former ZIPRA personnel, killing more than 100. This action prompted many ex- ZIPRA members to desert and go back to the bush with their guns. These desertions accelerated a year later when the government announced that it had uncovered arms caches on ZAPU-owned properties. Joshua Nkomo and the other ZAPU Ministers were sacked from the government and former ZIPRA leaders, notably Dumiso Dabengwa and Lookout Musuku, the deputy army commander, were arrested and charged with treason. They were later acquitted, but rearrested and detained without charge until 1986.* from early 1982 a military Task Force led by Lieutenant- Colonel Lionel Dyke, a former Rhodesian officer, was deployed in Matebeleland North against the ex-ZIPRA "dissidents," as the government called them. There were frequent reports of detention and torture of villagers. One eyewitness from Tsholotsho is reported as describing what happened when the Task force came to the village:

The soldiers beat and hit us and threatened us in a terrible was. They accused us of feeding dissidents. They hit one old woman and said that she was a mother of dissidents. Then the white soldier picked one boy and asked him what he was going to say. He said he knew nothing to say about dissidents. The white soldier took his gun from his belt and just shot the boy in the head. Just in front of us. *

In January 1983, the Task force was replaced by the Fifth Brigade, a unit which had been specially trained by North Korean military advisers and which was outside the normal command structure of the army, being directly under the control of the Prime Minister's office. The Brigade appeared to be almost exclusively composed of shona-speaking ex-ZANLA combatants. In the weeks followed, the Fifth Brigade carried out many killings of villagers in Matebeleland North. Reports indicated that often they visited villages with lists of ZAPU officials and sympathisers, who were singled out and killed.

They made little attempt to engage the "dissidents" militarily. There was an ugly strand of tribalism in the behaviour of the Fifth Brigade: the Ndebele were being punished for crimes their ancestors were supposed to have committed against the shona. Finally, in mid-1993, Mugabe responded to international pressure and withdrew the Fifth Brigade from Matebeland. A commission of inquiry was set up to investigate allegations of army abuses; although it submitted a report to the government, its findings were never public.

However, at the beginning of 1984, the Fifth Brigade was redeployed in Matebeleland South and the pattern of abuse was repeated. Again, there were reports of army killings and torture at a number of *ad hoc* army camps: Belaghwe, Sun Yet Sen. and Mphoengs. However, this time there was also a strict dusk to dawn curfew and restrictions on the movement of food into the area. This was the height of a severe drought, which affected the whole of Zimbabwe, but Matebeleland South worst of all. There had been some attempt to restrict food supplies in Matebeleland North in 1983 but now Operation Turkey was being wholeheartedly revived. Again, there was an international outcry and the Fifth Brigade was withdrawn. The journalist who played the greatest role in exposing the killings, Peter Godwin of the London *Sunday Times,* was expelled from the country. (Nick Worrall of *The Guardian* had been expelled the previous year.)

Exactly how many people died at the hands of the Fifth Brigade will never be known. The justice and Peace Commission stated in 1983 that it had gathered firm evidence of 469 civilian killings "for the most part by government soldiers." Clearly, the actual death toll was much higher- 1500 would be a conservative estimate.

A tiny handful of cases were security force members brought to justice for these killings. In June 1988, the four soldiers were among the 75 members of the security forces released under the amnesty.*

The initial "dissidents" were from the left wing of ZIPRA and had historically maintained strong links with the African National Congress of South Africa (ANC). Nevertheless, the South African government saw the instability in Matebeleland as a chance to pursue its own ends by arming and sponsoring its own "dissidents" bands. While the security forces were carrying out their abuses, the "dissidents" were committing their own atrocities against the civilian population and, on occasions, against others such as tourists and missionaries. One of the incidents, which grabbed international attention, occurred in November 1987 when "dissidents" hacked to death 16 members of a Protestant mission at Esigodini, including babies and small children. Such brutality affected the hapless people of Matebeleland for six years or so.

However, in certain instances there is evidence to suggest that killings were carried out by "dissidents" but by "pseudo-gangs" of the security forces. The tactics of impersonating guerrillas while committing atrocities was used by the Rhodesian forces in the independence war. In November 1985 Luke and Jean Khumalo, a Methodist headmaster and his wife, were killed at Thekwane School in Matebeleland South. The official version was that the dissidents were responsible. However, there were a number of unanswered questions.

Why did soldiers at an army camp three kilometres away not intervene, when the attackers were at the school for several hours, firing shots and burning buildings? The army did not even arrive when the school staff sent for help after the attackers had left. Why were the attackers wearing military uniform? In addition, why did they leave a note saying that?

Luke and Jean Khumalo were being killed for passing information to Amnesty International's call for an inquiry into the killings; the government stated that it had captured a member of the "dissident" band responsible. However, as far as Africa Watch can tell, no one has been charged with the murders.

In early 1985, a new pattern of human rights abuse emerged. Dozens possibly hundreds- of people throughout Matebeland and Midlands "disappeared as a result of night time abductions by armed men. The government's explanation was that the "disappeared people had gone to join the "dissidents" but there are a number of factors suggesting that the security forces were in fact responsible.

The victims were often middle-aged or old men - not the young men who might be expected to join the "dissidents." They were often driven away in vehicles - yet there are no recorded instances of "dissidents" having vehicles. On occasions, vehicles were identified as belonging to the security forces and sometimes the tracks were followed to the military camps. The armed men who came often spoke only poor Ndebele – the "dissidents" were usually fluent Ndebele speakers.* none of those abducted has reappeared since the "dissidents" were amnestied and came out of the bush in May 1988.

In late 1985, Amnesty International publicly stated its concern over torture in Zimbabwe. It followed this with a memorandum to the government detailing 21 cases of torture and seeking an impartial investigation. A report by the Lawyers Committee for Human Rights in May 1986 provided a more comprehensive review of the human rights situation. As with the expulsion of journalists who reported the Matebeleland killings, the government response was to blame the bearer of bad news. All allegations of torture were categorically denied. Amnesty International, which had adopted many members of the government as

"Prisoners of conscience" during their long spells in Rhodesian jails, was denounced as an "enemy of Zimbabwe." Former prisoner of conscience Robert Mugabe described it as "Amnesty Lies International," while home affairs Minister Enos Nkala (another Amnesty International alumnus) threatened to detain anyone who provided the organization with information. ***Is this how people are suppose to be treated after voting for a black majority, what is the difference between the Rhodesian rule of Zimbabwe and Zimbabwe rule?*** When you look at it is like a playground of evil people who have created their own experimental ritual research on animals, or even animals deserve better treatment as well. They are not allowed to exercise their human rights, the world is watching, Africa is watching, and so, what is next? Don't you wonder?

Furthermore, the Amnesty International never stopped fighting for human rights mechanism to be put in place but there was always a high huddle to jump for them. The December 1987 unity agreement was followed by a Cabinet reshuffle which brought ZAPU Ministers back into the government for the first time since 1982, but also removed the hard line anti-ZAPU Enos Nkala from the Ministry of Home Affairs and replaced him with Moven Mahachi. Soon after his appointment, Mahachi set about releasing the remaining Emergency Powers detainees. By April 1988 only a handful remained, who were released to mark the eighth anniversary of independence. Also on Independence Day Mugabe announced an amnesty for all those "dissidents" still in the bush who surrendered by the end of May. Some 113 did so and Matabeleland's security problems were largely at an end. Under the terms of the amnesty, none of those who surrendered could be prosecuted for crimes committed while they were in the bush. There was considerable popular discontent when "Gayigusu" – Morgan Sango Nkomo – took advantage of the amnesty. He had been responsible for the November

1987 massacre of the missionaries at Esigodini and other atrocities. Just to mention the least, because some of the other information is very sensitive if you are human enough and very sickening. I never thought in my whole life that some of these things were happening but after reading and talking to a number of people from all over Zimbabwe, I was shocked and felt sick and very disillusioned about the Zimbabwean government.

The other thing that I cannot come to terms with is the violation of rights to the payments of damages. On this Zimbabwe has a poor record. In 1986 Mugabe was questioned in Parliament about the government's failure to pay damages awarded against it unlawful arrest and detention. He replied: If government – and I want to say this as a matter of principle – were to be awarding damages and paying huge sums of money that are involved in these cases, some of which are of a petty nature, government would in my view be using the taxpayers' money wrongfully. It is true that government has not paid damages. Where, for example, a person suffers injury as a result of an accident involving on the one side, a vehicle driven by a government employee, we have paid- have not refused. However, where people take advantage of liberal situation to go to court and win on technicalities, they should not expect that the government is going to use the people's resources to enrich them when we believe in some cases that they are wrongdoers.*

It had apparently not occurred to the Prime Minister that the misuse of taxpayers' money came with the unlawful arrest, not the subsequent award of damages to the wronged parties. There is no legal remedy in Zimbabwe if the State refuses to pay damages awarded by the court. **

In any case, when one reads some of these issues involving human rights it becomes clear that there was never law laid out for the welfare of the civilians, the people, but the law had to be given in for the perpetrators, or the violators of the human rights. There was a clear indication that the government employees, especially the law enforcement group, soldiers, air force, police force. The people of Zimbabwe were practically exposed and as much as they would like to feel, they had a roof over their heads, but reading and researching has opened up my mind that there was no one to give people of Zimbabwe security that was eminent for them.

People of Zimbabwe feared to air their views, stopped their children to say anything that has to do with the government or else they will be maimed or killed or disappear forever. I can see through a wall in my memory that is how they lived, I can imagine even by trying to exercise their rights through the ballot box by voting during the elections times, they will still be maimed or killed. Because they are dealing with people who never had them at heart and treat them with respect, inhumane is the norm.

* Incidentally, the case of Dabengwa and Masuku also illustrates the folly of retaining former Rhodesian CIO officers. The ex-ZIPRA army officers who carried out the catching of arms appear to have a police agent working under the orders of Mart Calloway, the head of CIO in Hwange. Calloway later defected to South Africa where he became a crucial figure in organising support for the "dissidents". The continued detention of the two popular ZIPRA leaders was an important factor provoking anti-government sentiment in Matebeleland. Calloway's role is outlined in Joseph Hanion, "Destabilisation and the Battle to Reduce Dependence" in Colin Stoneman (Ed), *Zimbabwe's Prospects*, London 1988.

** "Rhodesian troops prop up Mugabe," *Africa Now*, July 1984.

* Article 2 (3) of the International Covenant on Civil and Political Rights

(Which Zimbabwe has not signed or ratified) amplifies the point:

Each State Party to the present Covenant undertakes:

(a) To ensure that any person whose rights or freedoms are as herein recognised are violated shall have an effective remedy, notwithstanding that the violation has been committed by persons acting in an official capacity;

(b) To ensure that any person claiming such remedy shall have his right thereto determined by competent judicial, administrative or legislative authorities, or by any other competent authority provided for by the legal system of the State, and to develop the possibilities of judicial remedy;

(c) To ensure that the competent authorities shall enforce such remedies when granted.

* Speech of July 16, 1986, cited in G Feltoe, *a Guide to Zimbabwe Cases Relating to Security, Emergency Powers and Unlawful arrest and Detention*, Legal Foundation, Harare 1988, pp8.

** *Ibid*, pp8-9

Chapter 8

Although the Justice and Peace Commission continued its work on behalf of detainees and their dependents, as well as bringing the High Court action on behalf of the dependents of "Disappeared" people from Silobela. The commission continues to submit details of its concerns confidentially to government, as well as making public statements on important human rights issues. Despite these occasional problems, the prestige of the Justice and Peace Commission has usually enabled it to carry out its investigations without official harassment.

At that moment, Zimbabwe was now in a position or rather appeared more open to investigations by international human rights organisations. In October 1988 there was a warm official welcome for a "Human Rights Now!" concert sponsored by Amnesty International in Harare and Zimbabwean officials have been ready to respond to Africa Watch's inquiries about detentions and other reported human rights abuses.

Another non-governmental organisation, the Legal Resources Foundation, set up in 1985, has been doing important work in making legal services and knowledge of legal rights accessible to a broader public. This has been achieved through publications, legal advice sessions and training programs. In April 1989, Bulawayo Legal Projects Centre, run by the foundation, began a training program for police and other law enforcement officers in various human rights aspects of criminal procedure.

With the advent of peace in Matabeleland, the situation in Mozambique poses the most serious threat to Zimbabwe's security and to the human rights of Zimbabweans. The threat is caused by the activities of the opposition guerrilla organisation RENAMO (Resistencia Nacional Mocambica – Mozambique National Resistance). RENAMO, which for nearly two decades has waged a brutal war against FRELIMO, the former liberation movement that forms the government of Mozambique, was now engaged in frequent attacks on Zimbabwe. However, the cause for concern in the eastern districts of Zimbabwe is not only RENAMO activities, but also the response of the Zimbabwean army. This sharply poses the question of whether the government and army have learnt the lessons of their disastrous mishandling of the Matabeleland crisis.

RENAMO has always been closely bound up with the internal politics of Zimbabwe. It was formed in the early 1970s by the Rhodesian CIO, primarily as a means of gathering intelligence on the Zimbabwean liberation organisation operating from Mozambique.* in the first instance RENAMO was recruited from among the Ndau, a shona-related ethnic group which straddles the border between south-eastern of Zimbabwe and Mozambique. Even today, much of the leadership of RENAMO is Ndau, including its top leader, Alfonzo Dhlakama, and it appears to draw greatest support in Shona-speaking areas of Mozambique. At Zimbabwe's independence in 1980, RENAMO "was transferred lock, stock and barrel" to the South African Military.* under South African control RENAMO rapidly changed from primarily an intelligence organisation to one wholly dedicated to sabotage and destabilization. RENAMO's creator Ken Flower later wrote: "I began to wonder whether we had created a monster that was now beyond control."**

In the first three years after Zimbabwean independence, the South African military also made at least a dozen direct attacks on Mozambique. These included a raid on the oil tank farm in Beira port by the Reconnaissance Commando in December 1982, which caused a major fuel crisis in Zimbabwe. There were a number of other attacks on Beira and the transport corridor to Zimbabwe, which was the country's main outlet to the sea other than through South Africa. In 1982, Zimbabwe committed a Special Task Force of the national army to guard the Beira-Mutare oil pipeline. The legal basis for the intervention was the 1981 Zimbabwe – Mozambique Defence Agreement. In 1984, Mozambique signed a pact with South Africa at Nkomati, whereby the latter would withdraw its support from RENAMO. However, RENAMO continued to grow in military strength, and Zimbabwean military involvement in Mozambique deepened. In 1985 Zimbabwean paratroopers captured the RENAMO base at "Casa Banana" in Gorongosa. Not only did this signal a deeper Zimbabwean troops found documents indicating continued South African support for RENAMO in violation of the Nkomati accord, including three visits to Gorongosa by the South Africa Deputy foreign minister. RENAMO responded to this increased Zimbabwean involvement by stepping up attacks inside Zimbabwe. In 1986, RENAMO announced that it was "declaring war" on Zimbabwe.

Zimbabwe government has minimized the extent of RENAMO activity within the country, largely for political reasons, since the army's involvement in Mozambique is far from universally popular.

RENAMO abuses within Mozambique have been well documented and have received wide international publicity.* the guerrillas have carried out frequent killings, including large-scale massacres, and horrific mutilations of civilians, by cutting off ears, lips, noses and fingers. It is not widely appreciated internationally that RENAMO is perpetrating similar acts in the eastern districts of Zimbabwe.

One of the great-unresolved issues further complicates the political situation in eastern Zimbabwe since independence: land. The importance of the land issue in the struggle for independence. However, since 1980 there has been no reform of the system of land tenure, nor a radical redistribution of land from the large-scale commercial farms to the land-hungry peasants in the communal areas. Manicaland is the area of the country where that pressure has most acute. When Africa Watch's delegate visited Zimbabwe in April 1989, he saw an example of the discontent caused by the land problem on a farm in the Cashel valley in Manicaland. Some 21 families (about 200 people) were camped there in squalid conditions – and in some danger of attack from RENAMO – after being evicted from land nearby Chimanimani. They constituted only about a quarter of the families evicted from two farms, Hangani and Sawerombi. The families from Hangani had owned the land before it had been taken by white settlers in the 1890s. They had been allowed to stay on the land as farm labourers until late 1988 when they were evicted under a court order obtained by the present owner.

The white owner had abandoned the other farm, Sawerombi, shortly after independence and families from the neighbouring communal areas had moved on to the land and farmed as a cooperative. In 1987, the same owner acquired the land. It appears that the land has been bought for speculative purposes rather than productive use; after independence this same farmer bought a number of farms in Cashel valley, which he resold to the government and Forestry Commission for a considerable profit in 1983. The Sawerombi "squatters" were also evicted in late 1988.*

It is apparent that in Manicaland there is the same explosive cocktail of destabilising factors, which led to such serious insecurity in Manicaland: armed insurgency organised political opposition and social grievances. What is most disturbing is that the government appears to be reacting in precisely the same manner to the RENAMO threat as it did to the dissidents in Matebeleland. Instead of making a clear distinction between legitimate political dissent and armed opposition, it is amalgamating ZUM, RENAMO and South Africa, in precisely the same manner as it did in Matebeland. If legal avenues of political opposition are closed, it is not inconceivable that popular support for RENAMO will grow.

To combat RENAMO the army in the border areas has revived an old tactic from the Smith years: the protected village. In all the areas worst affected by RENAMO attacks the civilian population is compelled to gather at night under army protection. In some areas, however, the local have complained that the protection provided is inadequate – in Rushinga, it is complained that in four years the army has failed to engage RENAMO. Some observers comment that the main purpose of the protected village policy is to separate Zimbabweans from Mozambican refugees and migrants.

Historically there have been large numbers of Mozambican migrant workers in eastern Zimbabwe, particularly on the large farms and the tea and sugar plantations. In those years the numbers swelled by refugees fleeing the political violence in Mozambique. Official figures put the number of refugees in camps at 75,000, with some 100,000 spontaneously settled elsewhere. Mozambicans in Zimbabwe have endured the most of the government's frustration at its inability to deter RENAMO attacks. According to refugee organisations, 8,000 to 9,000 Mozambicans were illegally and summarily expelled from Zimbabwe in 1988, usually on the allegation that they were RENAMO supporters and often in direct response to a particular RENAMO attack. In fact, expelled refugees have usually ended up in reception centres run by the Mozambican Government – suggesting that they were not RENAMO supporters. Refugee organisations say the Zimbabwean authorities have moderated their behaviour towards Mozambican refugees and that there have been fewer expulsions in 1989. However, they also comment that there is often a considerable gap between the enlightened attitudes of the civilian authorities and the behaviour of the army on the ground. Clearly, Mozambicans in Zimbabwe outside the refugee camps remain at risk.*

Africa Watch has also come across disturbing evidence of abuse by the Zimbabwean army against Mozambicans within their own country. Africa Watch has asked the Zimbabwe Government to conduct an urgent inquiry into the detention of about 35 Mozambicans, including small children, arrested in Espungabera on March 16, 1989. Those detained included the families of Pio Mutambara and Edmore Simango. In mid-April the Grey's Scouts in Mutandahwe, camp held them, inside Zimbabwe. ** They alleged that they had been tortured; a claim which was given substance by the fact that one of those detained had clearly suffered serious damage to his legs. They said that they expected to be transferred to Tongogara refugee camp, which suggests that they were not seriously suspected of being in contact with RENAMO.

Africa watch has received no reply to its inquiries about these prisoners. A number of informants have told Africa Watch that the Zimbabwean army is deliberately depopulating a wide swath of territory down the Mozambican side of the border and that many of those removed from their villages have been imprisoned inside Zimbabwe. Such claims are, by their nature, difficult to confirm. However, the case of the prisoners at Mutandahwe suggests that in at least one instance the allegation has substance.

* commenting on *Evans and another v Chairman of the Review Tribunal and another* HH-131-86, Feltoe writes:

This case lies down that it is incumbent upon the Minister of Home Affairs to justify

The detention. The degree of proof required is the same as that in a civil case, namely proof on a balance of probabilities. (However, the Supreme Court said that because personal liability is involved when it comes to detention, the degree of probability required is high...)

The of this is that the person representing the Minister at review hearing if obliged to lead sufficient evidence against the detainee so as to prove the case against him on a balance of probabilities, it still remains for the Tribunal to decide whether on the facts proven against the detainee there is a justifiable basis for him to continue to be kept in detention.)

(G Feltoe, *A Guide to Zimbabwe Cases relating to Security, Emergency Powers and*

Unlawful Arrest and Detention, Legal Resources Foundation, Harare 1988, p7.

** *Minister of Home Affairs & Another v Austin & Another* S-79-86

* *Manica Post,* June 30, 1989.

Chapter 9

Life is what happens to you, while you are busy making other plans. Whilst there still was no way to express my feelings about the deteriorating political and economical situation in Zimbabwe, I left the country for a better future. There are times when I had to refrain from writing this book due to feeling very uncomfortable with some of the issues that I have come across through my reading and researching. It makes me wonder, what was going on in my country. I sometimes feel sick, very worried and my trust of anybody who is a Zimbabwean are getting slimmer and slimmer. Due to, I do not know who is who at this present day and age. However, the fact is somewhere somehow, for the sake of the future generation one has to write about the atrocities that were caused by these manmade disasters of a country called Zimbabwe.

Let us get back to our stories of this country called Zimbabwe, since the formation of (ZUM) Zimbabwe Unity Movement. The leader of ZUM is a former secretary-general of ZANU-PF, Edgar Tekere. Tekere was removed from the party and government posts in 1981 after his acquittal on a technicality murdering a white farmer the previous year. However, Tekere remained influential among the left wing of the ruling party and particularly in his home are of Manicaland on the eastern border, where he was provincial party chairman. He criticized corruption and the size of government, as well as increasingly distancing himself from the move towards a one-party state. In early 1988, he was removed from the leadership of ZANU-PF in Manicaland. Then, in October 1988, he made a speech fiercely attacking government corruption. However, he went a step further than any previous critics did by placing some of the blame on Mugabe for failing to remove corrupt members of government. The Central Committee of ZANU-PF promptly voted to expel him.

The episode was revealed because the defenders of single-party systems argue that criticism can be contained and encompassed within the framework of the ruling party. Yet here was a demonstration that as soon as anyone overstepped an invisible line he would be removed. This was not intrinsically surprising: as early as 1985, a group of ZANU-PF trade unionists who criticised corruption among their union leadership were detained for some weeks. However, Tekere's expulsion did as much as any single episode to illustrate to ordinary Zimbabweans the dangers of the one-party state.

Tekere did not instantly follow the advice of his followers, who included a vocal group of students at the University of Zimbabwe, and set up a new party. By the time he finally did, Mugabe had made his own moves against corruption and taken some of the wind out of Tekere's sails. Publicly the ruling party declared itself unconcerned by the formation of ZUM, although many column inches in the government press were devoted to the new party has alleged links to die-hard Rhodesians and South Africa.

However, despite their professed indifference, the authorities instantly began a sustained campaign of harassment against ZUM. The first two months of its existence were particularly sensitive because they coincided with a parliamentary by-election in Harare's Dzivarasekwa constituency, which ZUM contested. The ZANU-PF candidate was declared to have won, with ZUM polling 28 per cent of the votes cast. Tekere alleged that two government ministers had illegally entered polling stations to intimidate voters, and that party loyalists had been bussed in from outside the constituency to vote. Africa Watch could not confirm these allegations. However, there must be serious doubts about the fairness of the election campaign. The police banned the first two ZUM election meetings at Highfield and Mabvuku – the first public meetings in the party's history –. A subsequent rally in Chitungwiza was called off because ZUM supporters were locked out of the stadium where it was to be held. The chairperson of Chitungwiza Town Council, Forbes Magadu, said that the gates were locked because ZUM had not paid a deposit. The Forbes Magadu is also ZANU-PF political commissar for Harare and plated a prominent part in the Dzivarasekwa campaign. At the same time security officials prevented members of the public from attending a meeting to launch ZUM in Bulawayo, and a ZUM official was subsequently charged with convening a public meeting without authority. A ZUM official also alleged that the managing director of the official Zimbabwe Newspapers had stopped an advertisement for a later ZUM rally in Bulawayo from appearing in the *Chronicle* newspaper.

On June 6, 1989 prominent ZUM member Freddie Madenge was arrested in Harare. Davison Gomo, a senior party spokesperson, Lazarus Matungwazi, James Dziva and 11 other members were arrested two days later. They were held without charge at Harare Central Police Station. Unusually, Home Affairs Minister Moven Mahachi responded publicly to Africa Watch appeals on behalf of the 15 detained ZUM members:

*"There is freedom to form political parties but there is no freedom to subvert a legitimate Government. We will not hesitate to pick anybody up as long as we have reasonable grounds that they are engaged in subversive activities."**

In fact, the 15 were released a few days later without charge, suggesting that the grounds for detaining them were not so reasonable. On July 18, 1989, Tekere was still trying to address his first public meeting since ZUM's formation. That evening armed police dispersed 5, 00 students who were attending a rally addressed by Tekere at the University of Zimbabwe. Police fired teargas into students' dormitories. On October 6-7, 1989, 11 ZUM members were arrested in Chinhoyi, some 70 miles from Harare. They included the party's provincial secretary for Mashonaland West, Cornelius Watama. At the time of writing, they had apparently not been charged and had not seen a lawyer. A ZUM spokesperson also alleged that a store owned by a party supporter had been stoned by members of the Youth League of the ruling party.

When a newly formed party can win nearly a third of the vote in ZANU-PF's Harare stronghold, President Mugabe may take this as evidence that the public is not yet won over the idea of the one-party state. However, it was worrying that in the first two months of the new party's existence it suffered repeated harassment and detentions. The government was apparently unaware of any contradiction between this and its verbal assurances that anyone is free to form a political party.

A development, which concerned some observers, was the transfer of responsibility for the Youth Wing and Women's League of the ruling party away from the relevant Ministries (Youth, Sport and Culture and Community and Women's Affairs) into the Ministry of Political Affairs. The fear was that in the period leading up to the next general election in 1990 these wings of the will be engaged in violence and intimidation of political opponents. Such fears are not fanciful, since this was precisely what happened around the last general elections in 1985. Supporters of ZAPU were forcibly bussed to ZANU-PF rallies, beaten up, had their homes burned down and in few instances where killed.*

Members of the Youth Wing were among those released under the June 1988 presidential amnesty. In September 1988, the Attorney General instructed the prosecution to drop all charges during trial of 13 youths from the ruling party alleged to have burned down and destroyed property owned by ZAPU members. The inference is that the government treats

such behaviour lightly. In a plural society, it is highly questionable whether such party bodies should fall under the control of any Ministry; at elections time it creates the appearance that supposedly impartial state organs are favouring one party against others.

Those who criticise from outside the framework of party politics scarcely fare better than members of minority parties do. In September 1988, students at the University of Zimbabwe and Harare Polytechnic attempted to organise a demonstration against corruption. However, the police prevented the demonstration from leaving the campuses and broke up the protests with teargas and baton charges. The demonstrators declared their loyalty to President Mugabe and were taken aback when he returned from an overseas trip to endorse the harsh police action. Law lecturer Shadreck Gutto, a Kenyan political exile, was summarily expelled from the country because he was alleged to have helped the students draft an anti-corruption manifesto. Four other lecturers, along with six students, were charged under the Law and Order (Maintenance) Act with inciting public violence. The charges were later dropped, but the 15 members of the University Students' Representative Council had their grants withdrawn by the government in January 1989, apparently because they had circulated documents, which were said to be offensive to the office of the President.

Two months later the grants were restored after the students wrote a letter of apology to the Minister of Higher Education. In many respects the withdrawal of the grants was a more serious sanction than the criminal charges. To cut off the students' means of livelihood was a harsher penalty than anything the courts were likely to impose. In addition, the criminal charges were unlikely ever to succeed in court, whereas the withdrawal of the grants was an administrative measure for which the authorities were not required to give a reason. The calculated humiliation of the students by their letter of apology do not enhance either intellectual freedom at the university or political freedom in the country at large.

In June 1989, one of the four lecturers, who had been charged, Kempton Makamure, acting Dean of the Faculty of Law, was arrested and detained for a week at Harare's Marimba police station. The Emergency Powers (Maintenance of Law and Order) Regulations require that written reasons for detention must be served within seven days of a person's arrest. Since Makamure was released just within that time limit, the reasons for his detention were never officially stated. Apart from his alleged involvement in the anti-corruption protest, Makamure had offended the government in May 1989 when he gave a radio interview to the official Zimbabwe Broadcasting Corporation criticising the country's new investment code. The code, which liberalised foreign exchange requirements for overseas companies and facilitated the repatriation of profits, was generally welcomed in Western economic circles but criticised by the Zimbabwean left. The two journalists who interviewed Makamure, Robin Shava and Nyika Bara, were suspended from their posts.*

On September 29, 1989, students at the university attempted to hold a seminar to mark the first anniversary of their anti-corruption demonstration.

Some 200 riot police and CIO members arrived on campus to disperse 300 students, telling them that their gathering was illegal. On October 2 1989, the Students' Representative Council (SRC) issued a statement protesting the police action as a violation of academic freedom. In the early hours of October 4, 1989, police again came onto the campus to arrest Arthur Mutambara, SRC president, and Enock Chikweche, the organization's secretary general. Mutambara was injured trying to escape arrest. As news of the arrests spread, thousands of students assembled to protest, according to reports in the government-owned press. In the course of this spontaneous demonstration, a Mercedes Benz car belonging to Vice-Chancellor Walter Kamba was damaged. At least 70 students were arrested. Later the same day Professor Kamba announced that the university was being closed indefinitely, the first time this had happened since independence in 1980. Kamba, who is known to be a close advisor of Mugabe, refused to condemn either the initial police action against the seminar or the arrest of the student union officials. Students were given only a few hours to leave the campus. The term had only just started and students had not yet received their grant payment, so many were stranded in Harare with no money. The closure, carried out in consultation with President Mugabe who is chancellor of the university, drew condemnation from the University Teachers' Association and the University Senate. Most of the students arrested on October 4 had been released by the end of the week, but six remain in detention at the time of the writing. Apart from the two SRC officials, they are Christopher Giwa, Peter Myabo, Edmore Tobaiwa and Samuel Simango. They were apparently held under the 30-day detention orders issued under the Emergency Powers (Maintenance of Law and Order) Regulations at various police stations in the Harare area.

Following that, there was the labour rights issue. Trade union rights, particularly for the black majority, were severely curtailed before independence. There has been a significant growth in trade unionism since 1980 and the emergence of a single trade union confederation, the Zimbabwe Congress of Trade Unions, which was often critical of government policy. However, under the 1985 Labour Relations Act the right to strike remains limited by lengthy negotiating procedures which must be exhausted before a strike can be regarded as legal.* the most serious threat to workers' rights lies in the prohibition under several different laws, including the Labour Relations Act, of the right of workers in "essential services" to withdraw their labour.

As in other areas, the Zimbabwean Government inherited repressive laws enacted by the Rhodesian regime, which it has since added to. The Emergence Powers Act defined essential services as hospitals, transport, electricity, water, sewerage, food fuel, coal fire brigade, coal mining and communications. These can be widened by notice in the Government Gazette. A notice of 1965, which is still in force, defines all finance, commerce and industry as essential services. The Law and Order (Maintenance) Act, dating from 1960, prescribes a maximum of five-years prison sentence for incitement to strike in an essential service (section 32) and ten years for interfering with an essential service (section 34).

In May 1989, junior doctors went on strike throughout the country in protest at pay and conditions of service. Many were arrested and 77 of them charged under sections 32 and 34 of the Law and Order (Maintenance) Act, although charges were later withdrawn after Mugabe himself had intervened to defuse the situation. However, as an apparent consequence of the doctors' strike, the government introduced new regulations under the Emergency Powers Act, which like the Law and Order (Maintenance) Act, outlaw strikes in "essential services." Since the definition of essential services in force is still that of the 1965 government notice, in effect any worker who goes on strike can be charged under the Emergency Powers (Maintenance of essential Services) Regulations, 1989, and will face a prison sentence of up to two years.

In August 1989, the new regulations were tried out for the first time against striking railway artisans. Then technicians at the Posts and Telecommunications Corporation (PTC) in Harare went on strike over a pay grievance. Telecommunications workers elsewhere in the country began a go-slow. By the first week in September, 116 PTC employees had been arrested and charged with breach of the new regulations. The lawyer for some of the accused argued that the regulations were in breach of the constitutional provision prohibiting forced labour.

As with the use of detention without trial, this appears to be an abuse of the use of emergency powers. The striking telecommunications workers have no connection with either the insurgency in Manicaland or South African espionage – the two stated reasons for maintaining the emergency. One leading PTC striker, Lovemore Matombo, was detained for a week under the Emergency Powers (Maintenance of Law and Order) Regulations and released just before the authorities were required to provide written reasons for his imprisonment.

After the closure of the university on October 4, the zi9mbabwe Congress of Trade Unions issued a statement condemning the act of the Vice-Chancellor and government, under the name of its general secretary Morgan Tsvangirai. On the morning of October 6, the CIO arrested Tsvangirai; later that day he was taken, barefoot and handcuffed, to his office, which the CIO officials proceeded to search. He was taken away and, at the time of writing had not been seen again. On October 11, the High Court issued an order compelling the CIO to give Tsvangirai's lawyer access to him within 24 hours. Shortly after Tsvangirai's arrest, two other senior union officials were briefly detained for questioning. They were Andrew Ganya, organising secretary of Plastics, Chemical and Allied Workers Union and Trust Ngirande, organising secretary of the National Leather workers' Union.

* In 1987 the government's Secretary for Labour is reported as saying: "All strikes since I took office have been illegal because I have not approved any Strikes." Cited by Brian Wood, "Trade Union Organisation and the Working Class" in Colin Stoneman (Ed), *Zimbabwe's* Prospects, Macmillan, London 1988, p304.

As an observer from afar, I think I am allowed to comment, since this is my democratic right. This is how Tsvangirai managed to mobilise people especially the young generation of Zimbabwe from all walks of life and all the most qualified occupants, who realised where he was coming from. On every workers' day holidays there were rally has to commemorate the successes of companies and their trade records. The other issue was that they supported all the workers on their day-to-day grievances at work. This made him very popular with the working force and students at higher learning institutions.

By the look of it this is a clear testimony that someone somehow, had this inclination of all the mismanagement of the government and as for Edgar Tekere, it is a pity no one took this man serious. He never minced his words; he said everything as it was in the government. He became very unpopular. Nevertheless, what can we say now?

The issue of Freedom of the press in Zimbabwe. In February 1989 Geoffrey Nyarota, editor of the official *Chronicle* newspaper in Bulawayo, found himself promoted to the newly created post of group public relations officer in Harare. The *Chronicle* had exposed a major corruption in which government ministers were buying cars from Harare's Willowvale assembly plant and reselling them at vast profit above the legal controlled price. As a result, President Mugabe set up a judicial commission of inquiry, which led to the resignation of several ministers.

Nyarota's deputy at the *Chronicle*, Davison Maruziva, was also promoted to become deputy editor of the *Herald* in Harare, which has been uncritical of any aspect of government policy or behaviour. The *Chronicle* has published no more corruption scoops under its new editor, Stephen Mpofu.

Under Nyarota and Maruziva, the *Chronicle* had provided chapter and verse for the allegations of corruption made by the students and Edgar Tekere. They were immensely popular and difficult to sack. Instead, they were subjected to what one backbench Member of Parliament called "elimination by promotion."

Almost inevitably, the Willowvale car scandal was dubbed "Willow-gate." It became known quite by accident in October 1988. Bulawayo businessman Obert Mpofu, who is also a member of parliament, received an unexpected cheque for nearly $4,000 from the Willowvale Company. It was actually intended for one Alford Mpofu, an employee of Mmnilal Naran who is a close friend of the then Industry Minister Callistus Ndlovu. (Naran had bought a $60,000 Bulawayo house for his friend, who was the minister responsible for the government-owned Willowvale plant. He was later arrested for foreign exchange offences.)

Alford Mpofu and another Naran employee, Don Ndlovu, had been allocated Mazda pick-up trucks from Willowvale on Naran's behalf. They had paid in advance but when they went to collect them, Mpofu had been allocated a cheaper model. Hence the refund, which was sent to the wrong Mpofu.*

The exposure of "Willowgate" was not apparent intended to embarrass the government, since both the original source and the journalist responsible are thoroughly loyal to Mugabe. Obert Mpofu, a government member of parliament, took his story to Nyarota, a former Mugabe press secretary. The *Chronicle* pursued the affair vigorously over the weeks that followed, publishing lists of ministers who had been allocated Willowvale vehicles – and details of how these were resold illegally for two or three times the official price. Apart from the Industry Minister Ndlovu, those implicated included two of Mugabe's most senior advisers: Minister of Defence Enos Nkala and Senior Minister for Political Affairs Maurice Nyagumbo.

Most Zimbabweans have a healthy scepticism towards the official news media, but retain a voracious appetite for real news. The *Herald's* dismissal record for serious reporting has led to a flourishing of independent news magazines such as *Parade* and *Prize Africa*, which mix sport, fashion and showbiz gossip with serious political journalism. The country's three daily papers, the *Herald*, the *Chronicle* and the *Manica Post*, are all government controlled, as are the *Sunday Mail* (Harare) and the *Sunday News* (Bulawayo) and two Shona and Sindebele weeklies. The weekly *Financial Gazette* is independent and critical, but has a small print run and is aimed largely at the white community.

The Catholic monthly magazine *Moto* is perhaps the most important forum for critical ideas. There is undoubtedly the market for a non-government daily newspaper with an independent editorial line. However, the existing dailies run at a loss and are heavily subsidised. There was no financial supporter prepared to incur the government's wrath by launching a new paper. Thus, the most important print media remain under effective government control. The radio, which is the most important news medium in a predominantly rural society with low-level literacy, is tightly controlled. Thus, the emergence of Nyarota's *Chronicle* as an investigative newspaper won it an enthusiastic readership in Harare, as well as Bulawayo. As the Willowvale story developed, long queues would form in the capital to wait the *Chronicle's* mid-morning arrival.

In November, the Chronicle was engaged in a further clash with government. A reporter, Gibbs Dube, accompanied by a driver named Phillip Maseko, visited the home of the governor of Matebeleland South, Mark Dube, to interview him about illegal gold-mining in Esigodini. (The two Dubes are not related.) the interview had been arranged by Geoffrey Nyarota. When they had seen the governor, Gibbs Dube and Maseko began the drive back to Bulawayo. Mark Dube's car overtook them and the governor and his security men flagged them down, seized their car keys and ordered them into his vehicle. They were driven to the governor's house. Gibbs Dube said afterwards:

The governor accused me of trying to discredit him. He accused me of publishing sensational news, which he said was not true. Then he started to assault me. He hit me twice with a clenched fist. He then tried to throw a beer bottle at me, but was restrained by one of the two men who were in the house. Then he left for his bedroom where he said he was going to fetch his gun to shoot me so that there would be big news to write about. He then came for me again, but his friends restrained him. Then he went for Cde Maseko and started assaulting him with his fist. At that point, I ran away and escape. *

Maseko was handed over to the custody of the Esigodini police, who held him for some hours – while denying to the *Chronicle* that they had any knowledge of him.

All this was too much even for the management of Zimbabwe Newspapers. The group's chief executive, Elias Rusike, observed that if Mark Dube went unpunished, "Zimbabwe maybe entering a new frightening era when the rights of ordinary citizens are trampled underfoot willy-nilly by that in authority."** Likewise deputy commissioner of police Douglas Chingoka criticised police at Esigodini for detaining Maseko on Governor Dube's orders: "The police should protect people and should not get unlawful orders as no one is above the law,"***

Mugabe's reaction was quite different. He spent a press conference attacking "over zealous" reporters and repeating Mark Dube's extraordinary allegation that the two *Chronicle* men had gone to the governor's house secretly, disguised as gardeners.

"A governor must be dignified," Mugabe said, "but this does not mean that there was no provocation."****

In September 1989, a Bulawayo magistrates' court found Governor Dube guilty of assault and fined him $150. at about the same time Joseph Polizzi, a reporter who had covered "Willowgate" for the Chronicle's sister paper, the Sunday News, narrowly escaped when a car drove at him as he left the office one night. He suffered bruising. Previously Polizzi had been arrested after he had dressed as a doctor in an attempt to enter Bulawayo city morgue to investigate a story. Polizzi alleges that he was assaulted and was suing the police. He was detained for eight days without charge.*

A fortnight after the Dube assault, Davison Maruziva telephoned Enos Nkala, the Minister of Defence, to seek his reaction to allegations that he was involved in the Willowvale racket. Nkala's response was quoted at length;

Where did you get that information? That information is supposed to be with the police and the president. I want that information here in my office. Who do you think you are?

If you do not travel here {to Harare}, I will teach you a lesson. I will use the army to pick you up and then you can ask your questions; I do not care...

Do not play that kind of game with me. I am not {Callistus Ndlovu.. I am not the kind to play with. Play with anybody else. I am giving you ultimatum: if by tomorrow you do not come back to me to say you are coming, then you will come by other means.

I have the power. I will lock you up. Along with your editor who gave you that information. That question must be answered. I am the acting Minister of home affairs, I am instructing the police to search your offices, and you can write that. *******

From the safety of hindsight, this sounds like bluster. Nkala lied to the commission of inquiry into corruption and was forced to resign. At the time however, since the Minister of Home Affairs was out of the country, Nkala was in charge of both army and police. He threatened in 1986 that anyone who sent information to Amnesty International would be locked up. In addition, to prove that he meant it he ordered the detention of the head of Zimbabwe's leading human rights organization. Just two weeks beforehand, a member of the government had beaten up a reporter and apparently got away with it. Maruziva was entitled to feel scared.

Nyarota later related, in sworn testimony to the commission of inquiry.

Some people came to warn us personally that this was no longer for us and in fact in due course the chairperson of the Zimbabwe Mass Media Trust [the major shareholder in Zimbabwe Newspapers] summoned me to Harare and indicated that reaction was very strong at this point from certain government ministers.

He told me he had called me up for my safety, that he understood that there were instructions that I should be first dismissed from work and subsequently arrested. He called me to Harare so that I would be safe here.

I did confirm that Callistus Ndlovu, who; while the Information Minister had been away had been appointed acting minister, had issued instructions to the Zimbabwe Mass Media Trust that I should be dismissed immediately, which move the trust resisted.******

*   *The Herald, November 28, 1988.*

**   *The Herald, November 29, 1988*

*** *The Herald, November 30, 1988*

**** *Ibid.*

*****The *Chronicle*, December 14, 1988.

******The *Chronicle*, January 27, 1989.

At the end of December, Mugabe finally appointed a commission of Inquiry, headed by Justice Wilson Sandura, although there was still a widespread view that it would be a white wash. As it turned out, the commission held well-attended and highly theatrical hearings in Harare, where ministers such as Nkala and Ndlovu endured a merciless public inquisition. By the time the commission had reported, five ministers and a provincial governor had been forced to resign. One minister, Maurice Nyagumbo, committed suicide by drinking pesticide.

This should have been Nyarota's hour of glory. However, in January- shortly after the Sandura commission was established – information Minister Witness Mangwende announced his intention of "examining the structures" of the Mass Media Trust. Restructuring, it soon emerged, simply meant moving Nyarota and Maruziva where they do no harm. Nyarota was moved to a previously unheard of public relations job and Maruziva soon followed him to Harare. Formally, of course, these were promotions. But even Mugabe himself, seemed to have difficulty in getting his story straight. He said that no one would complain about getting a higher salary, but at the same time criticized Nyarota for "over zealousness." However, if Mugabe was uncertain whether Nyarota's removal was punishment or reward, the message conveyed to the public was clear Nyarota was promoted because he went too far.

Nyarota's removal aroused considerable public concern. Backbench Member of Parliament Byron Hove raised the matter in the House of Assembly. Ministers closed ranks, repeating the universal refrain of the government censor: they did not object the criticism, but it had to be constructive. Thus Sydney Sekeramayi, the Minister of State for National Security: "I want to stand here and make it very clear that some of us do not condone corruption, we are with it. But to the extent that the press now deliberately target Government as its enemy, then we part ways."*

In the course of his contribution to the parliament debate on Nyarota's removal, Byron Hove quoted from a pamphlet by Mikhail Gorbachev. "Criticism is a bitter medicine, but the ills that plague society make it a necessity. Those who think that criticism need only be dosed out at intervals are wrong. People who are inclined to believe stagnation has been fully overcome and it is time to take it easy are just as wrong. A slackening of criticism will inevitably harm *glasnost* and *perestroika*."** A few weeks later Hove was advertised to address the Britain-Zimbabwe Society on the theme of "The need for *glasnost* and *perestroika* in Zimbabwe." The meeting never took place, after ZANU-PF Politburo member Didymus Mutasa had intervened to stop it.

Nyarota is the third editor to be removed from his post for offending the government. His removal, like the previous ones, raises important questions about who controls the press in Zimbabwe. At independence in 1980, the government, with the help of a Nigerian grant, bought out south African owners of the *Herald, chronicle* and *Manica Post* and their Sunday counterparts and set up a Mass Media Trust as principal shareholder in Zimbabwe Newspapers (1980) Ltd. The trustees are supposed to represent the people of Zimbabwe and trust objects strenuously when the newspapers are described as government-owned. However, in practice it is clear that the Minister of Information plays the decisive role in hiring and firing senior staff.

In July 1985 Elias Rusike, head of Zimbabwe Newspapers, wrote to Willie Musarurwa, removing him from the editorial chair at the *Sunday Mail*, Henry Muradzikwa, ran a story about Zimbabwean students being deported from Cuba allegedly because they were suffering from AIDS. The story coincided with the visit to Harare of a top Cuban official who objected to it. Mugabe publicly pledged, "I shall deal with him personally." Muradzikwa, like Nyarota, was removed to a non-editorial post. The Mass Media Trust does not seem to have been consulted.

On May 18, 1989 Robin Shava and Nyika Bara of the Zimbabwe Broadcasting Corporation interviewed Kempton Makamure on the new investment code for the Radio 4 program entitled "Gate." According to Byron Hove, who subsequently raised the matter in parliament, the following day the journalists were hauled up before Information Minister Mangwende and asked why they had "picked on Makamure who is in opposition to Government." In a letter from the Senior Controller of Radio Services, the two were suspended from duties with effect from May 23. **

Replying to Hove, Mangwende's Deputy Kenneth Manyonda made the customary disclaimer of government involvement in the suspensions, but then told the parliament, "it is not that Code should not be criticized, but that it should be criticized knowledgeably." He went on: "Any journalist who is worth his salt should know that there are two sides to any story, and considering that the Investment Code is what everybody was waiting for it was only proper for the press to play its role positively by giving those involved equal and ideally the first opportunity to inform and educate the public." *** This was a curious comment, given that the press had spent the previous few weeks giving code enthusiastic mentions at every opportunity. The interview with Makamure was probably the first contrary view to be heard in the official media, Makamure's prior involvement with students' criticism was presumably not a coincidence. Hove pressed Manyonda on whether Shava and Bara were not in fact suspended because they held views critical of the government on the investment code issue. Manyonda would not confirm that the two journalists were summoned before the Minister on May 19 but did say that: *All I am aware of is that when we listened to the tapes that involved the interviews on Radio 4 we were so perturbed that we brought the situation to the attention of ZBC management. What they did later, quite honestly we do not know.* ****

According to an unconfirmed report, Shava and Bara were later reinstated and, like Nyarota promoted out of harm's way.

The exposure of "Willowgate" was an outstanding achievement by the young Zimbabwean press. It was able to occur largely because of the December 1987 unity agreement. The result has been a new era of political openness a breakdown in traditional party alignments. But now it appears that the opportunity for dissent was only temporary. The *Chronicle* has returned to bland predictability. The *Herald,* under Editor Tommy Sithole, continues to ignore financial scandals and to pour scorn on government critics. In April, after one particular partial *Herald* report about Edgar Tekere, a former political prisoner and veteran of the liberation struggle wrote an open letter to Sithole.

Lack of information and the absence of straightforward reporting are the direct causes of rumour-mongering. A pertinent example of this was the failure of the Herald to report Willowgate until the President announced the appointment of the Sandura Commission of Enquiry. This lack of reporting in the Herald was naturally widely commented on giving rise to the rumour that Tommy Sithole is himself implicated in Willowgate."...

Without accurate and untarnished information, it is difficult for people to make correct decisions and this, at the end of the day, can damage the State.... However, just as people demand and eventually get a certain standard in the conduct of Government, so people demand and eventually get a certain standard in the press that serves them. That is what the struggle for press freedom is all about. ****

* *Zimbabwe: Parliament Debates,* February 15, 1989.

** *Ibid.*

*** *Zimbabwe: Parliament Debates,* May 30, 1989.

*****Zimbabwe: Parliament Debates,* May 31, 1989.

Chapter 10

The thing is, life is how you make it most of the time and us who are away from the motherland in Africa, it is a process that will come to pass. I left my country not knowing that one day I will be here for a very long time, I mean a long time than expected. As I left Zimbabwe, I thought that I would one-day return home after working abroad and achieving better qualifications in order to have a better life style. Not knowing that I was going to be here for some time, I mean a good long time with uncertain tomorrow. It seems its survival of the fittest, well I was a coward then, I could not bear the stigmata of being humiliated and looked down upon, and the fact remains, that I was harassed for being a woman with an open mind.

Well I am not against anybody but I think when opportunities come they should let women also have the same chances just like men. Fortunately, my sixth sense always led me in the right path. Well for the sake of my sixth sense, I had to leave just in time to be a future reference to the future of Zimbabwean history with the little that I can share with you, as you read this book.

My leaving or rather my departure was based on, my earnings not meeting the life necessities, like just affording a loaf of bread, for thy self-alone. Fortunately or unfortunately, I remember this vividly when my mother commented on my frequent visits, that is when I moved out and tried to live own my own. As usual, my Saturday's were to the township, back to my roots, to mom, around two-thirty in the afternoon, on the dot, I will be opening the gate, and my mom would say it is she, and really, that was I!

One day my mom, Said to me, "You who went to live under those bright lights right at the heart of the town centre, the capital city where you can live on hamburgers and chips, so why have you come to the township where we are living on vegetables and our special maize meal dish sadza". It was so embarrassing, but deep down I understood my mother she had all the love for me and my not coming meant that I was starving in my studio flat. Well tell me who does not want to grow-up, look after their mother and thy self. It's more like, I would give her today a few dollars tomorrow I am there to help her eat the food she will have bought with the money I had given her a few days ago. What an embarrassment!

I came to Europe with one thing in mind, to advance my qualifications, for greener pastures, thinking maybe things would work out well for me, when I return back home. Well since I have been working my *** out maybe, maybe I will get there. However, one thing for sure I will not go there as long as there is no democracy. As an observer from afar, the thing that I have observed is, Zimbabweans are keen observers of any poor condition economically, politically and they are not shy to take advantage of it when it shows weakness.

I think now, I understand politics better than before. I never expected anything along this line to happen to my country, Zimbabwe. Tell me, who does not like Zimbabwe. Tell me; even British people still love our country, Zimbabwe. I managed to engage into my studies that I have always wanted. I am studying a web-master course in an open learning college. I do not know how things are going to work out. At present, I can manage to look after my family without going there to help her eat the food she will have bought with the money that I will have send her.

When the economy of Zimbabwe started deteriorating, the young working force of Zimbabwe started to migrate. What would anyone expect people to do, besides to seek?

Alternative solutions, leave the country? Zimbabwean started moving out of the country carrying their knowledge, which was needed for the development of the country. The big people (executives) started to help themselves and their families in taking money; little knowledge is dangerous, because some people thought they would get away with it.

This is just an outburst of wishing things could have been laid out such a manner that we would not trust anyone with the government funds with anyone. Did we try to maintain our relationship with the International Nations? No! Why? Who cares! Heard that saying, "make hay whilst the sun is still shining" that is a fact, it is either you take it or leave it. Although, when they look at the British in general, they did went on a serious business, "colonization" all over the world, especially Africa for its richness in minerals and the soil which was good for cultivation, and there is life in Africa. There is no hurry in Africa.

As a thinker, my own views, I suppose, the administration of the country (Zimbabwe) failed to work due to lack of some knowledge, due to people on the top being self-centred not willing to learn, because we fought the war, yes, a very big Yes! Our brothers and sisters perished for this country, but did that gave anyone to grind the country's economy to this state, which it is in. On the other hand, a country's economy is not based on personalising country's economical issues, but it needs support from every angle, meaning from top to bottom, then vice-versa. Not knowing that the repercussions were going to make the country go on an economic sliding down scale and no coming back.

It's like a car without good brakes on a slop going down, you cannot stop it because it will overturn, you cannot risk that, but you just hold on and pray for a miracle to happen, No reverse! That is the current economic status of our country today. Prices on basic commodities sky rocketing.

Many people were misled to the understanding of independence of our country. Whereby many Zimbabweans thought that, it was leisure time not knowing that we actually needed to work twice as much in order to achieve our goals, to have a strong economic background, you find that most people started stealing long time ago and it was more of a habit. Moreover, people started to look at where do you come from why should you have such a post when no one from you area was a minister or a prominent supporter of the current ruling part. We were ruled out as a backbencher. Bureaucracy creped in slowly and it was openly exposed.

Well, my fellow citizens, this is a very sad story about Zimbabwe; we use to laugh at Zambia, Malawi, Mozambique, you name it. Tell me where are we now? Scattered all over the world as lost cattle no one intend to find us besides setting our minds on the consoling fact that, "I am in Europe". I think we need to go back to the **drawing board, and start all over again. Let us try to find ourselves and remember there is no place like home. We are very educated people, but we lack this other thing called," Togetherness". We do not feel for one another. Do you remember, our freedom fighters' words, Child of the soil!** There were their ancestors of Zimbabwe, the true leaders who were not going to let us down. Because their love of people was greater than you can think, it was there but time was not on their side in life.

There was always a disturbance when they try to come up with something to construct our country. Therefore, if you are not observant, I want you to try to look at all the people you emulate and tell me what you see in their eyes. Because that's where all the personality of a person is whom you emulate or hate or who can be a leader, "eyes don't lie", take my word.

Us walking on this earth, are we the god's saints who want to preach the political gospel of Zimbabwe. By the look of it, we can talk in our small gatherings, have a lot to say, but do we take it further than that besides to saying I am not political. Do you even ask yourself that you are not in your country you have seek refuge, one day you should go back home. Well, I suppose our fellow British did not understand the reason behind Zimbabweans coming to this country. On the other hand, it showed solidarity, or patriotism of black and white Zimbabweans protesting against what is happening in the country. It rather confuses me in a way. Nevertheless, I think my confusion is in the way we are confused and do not know what we want maybe. The colonisation also played its part because Zimbabweans are lay back people just like the British. The mannerism is the same.

Let me take you back again the honeymoon period, Zimbabwean independence. Huh! Let us look back my friends. Soon after independence there was a lot that happened so fast so much that to those who liked slow move, they were left behind. It was more of a freedom train just get on board, no questions asked either thinking was necessary. We started moving into the areas, 'white suburban' that were previously owned by the white people, suburban homes, schools our kids were now enjoying the white people's schools. The facilities were wonderful and very well equipped. We had what we never had before.

A Black-man for a Head Master, and Head Mistress in a multi-racial school. At that moment, we were mixed and everything seems to be blending in well. Everything was a dream come true for every Zimbabwean! Hey! It was more of a prestige to be asked where your kids are going to school, and you say, "Prince Edward" with that English accent that we had acquired, we use to call it, "the nose brigade", and we felt we were more British than the British themselves, speaking through the nose. People preferred to buy their groceries in town centre those days at OK's departmental stores or TM you name it. It was very trendy. After all that, you get in a taxi to go as far as Highfield, which was more than 20miles.

After a few years' signs of deterioration to a number of things started showing, like the maintenance of government buildings. Most of us now had our kids in the group 'A' schools no restrictions. You would take your daughter or son wherever you want, depending on your pocket. It was too rosy, and very artificial as far as," miss observant", is concerned. Other people it was genuine because they were working very hard to earn the hard cash. I believe in the Russian saying, "In order for you to develop in either way, you need to take three steps ahead and then two steps backwards". I hope you will get me properly there. I mean for any plans in general you can try to implement this method, which means we need to learn from history and learn to listen. You lose nothing in listening because it might sound nonsense, but in the end, it can be a good idea.

Let us get back to the historical events of our country, Zimbabwe. Before independence, Mugabe's ZANU-PF made clear its intentions that Zimbabwe should be a one-party state. The independence construction agreed with Britain at Lancaster House in 1979 guarantees the preservation of a multi-party political system until 1990 – 10 years after independence unless all members of parliament agree to it. For his party, President Mugabe said that a one-party system will not be introduces without popular support.

The move towards a one-party system has considerable symbolic importance for defenders of Rhodesia, who like to maintain that the maintenance of institutionalized racism was in fact a defence of western democratic values against Marxist tyranny- as if those values could be reconciled with the refusal to count persons equally because of race. However, this

does not have wide currency among Zimbabwe's remaining white population of around 100,000. Mugabe's government has assiduously wooed the whites because of the significant economic role. During that period, a number of white farmers joined ZANU-PF, at the national level, Mugabe has succeeded in attracting the support of long-standing members of Ian Smith's Rhodesian Front, notably former Justice Minister Chris Anderson, and

Charles Duke, both of whom hold ministerial posts. In 1987, at the earliest opportunity constitutionally available to it, the government introduced an important democratic reform by abolishing the 20 per cent of parliamentary seats reserved exclusive for whites. Although there was no general election held at that moment, any political party, including a one with a predominantly white membership, was entitled to contest any parliamentary seat.

The never-ending decline of the Zimbabwean economy has been mostly entirely due to government's act of commission and of omission. **The Zimbabwean government did not solicitude the foundation of the economy, agriculture, through its comprehensible ill-conceived basis of attaining much-needed land reform and through near-criminal mismanagement.**

The government's policies and actions did more to fuel hyperinflation than any other causes. Through the government abuses of international recognised fundamental principles of human rights, justice, law and order and respect for property rights, compounded by a continuous barrage of vitriolic insults targeted to many of the international countries.

The Zimbabwean government vigorously discouraged foreign direct investment and provoked the withholding of the much needed developmental aid and balance of payment support. By the government rigid resistance to extensive privatisation of parastatals and its unwillingness or inability to fund parastatals adequately, concurrently with unwillingness to effect meaningful managerial appointments in many of them, the infrastructural support base of the economy has collapsed and still collapsing more and more, with inadequate availability of energy, disastrously ineffectual telecommunications and much else retarding economic activity. To any educated person this declining of a country's economy clearly showed that there was no future no life.

Chapter 11

Working in Europe, and leaving our professional jobs in Zimbabwe. We are settled, working like those foreigners who came to Zimbabwe. Working in England, I have been trying to solve a puzzle here, as usual. I am being my old self-observant. Observing from afar, I have been working with my fellow citizens of Zimbabwe, when you listen to their conversation, it is more of money nothing else. People do hard work, I tell you, I have seen it with my eyes. They do not have a life; they do not even know where they are coming from or going. A conversation that you can have with them is only to talk about money; well I tell you I do not work like that because it is not necessary. I look at what they have achieved in life, nothing, at all, so why bother.

They only know how to blame, other people nothing more. If you try to talk the political economic status of our country, they are a bit interested, they can switch their mind off let it go quicker than you expect. They work day in day out. This has become a playground for families breaking-up for more divorces than you can think of. Women are now becoming bigamists, a husband here another one in Zimbabwe. Just as well, men do the same. Married woman put up with British men trying to run away from paying rent, bills. Others strippers in the streets at night, so that they can be able to get money to send home.

Be very careful with the money you receive from Europe, because you will never know what you are going to receive next, if not a corpse then a terminal ill person. Some are HIV positive dying each day, if not spreading it. This is not because I am single; I have a lot of respect on myself. I am a one-man woman. Unbelievable! Others are doing very well changed their professions. They are now serious professionals earning a good salary have a very good life with their wives or husbands

Others are struggling in the right direction advancing their previous professions they have a hope that things will change one day, then we will go back home. **Heard that saying," Human beings are the last species on earth and the worst".** This is true, let us look at the respect of human nature in general; People are dying each day, and endless wars. I have been thinking which other country in Africa that never had a problem, politically neither economically. Which one, can someone let me know? Well it seems one way or the other. We have had a fair share of it all as blacks and just as well being from the black continent, in Europe.

The impression that the Zimbabweans are keen observers of the condition known as democracy and are not shy of taking advantage of it when it shows weakness. Fellow citizens of Zimbabwe in the land of the survival of the fittest were qualifications are long forgotten only survival of the fittest is the norm, the routine of life style in Europe. I have been observing my fellow citizens, since some of us were not doing any manual labour at home; it seems we cannot catch-up, with our fellow citizens. I mean those we use to be in charge of at work, some of us we were managers, director's you name it. In the land of survival you are all at par, and it is highly likely that they get more than you do they can work 60-80hours a week.

What I enjoy more than anything is to sit afar watch how some struggles to try to catch up with them. I am fortunate that I grew up under good situation that we use to do all in the form of labouring ourselves, thus when the upbringing contributes.

A big thanks to my mother, for that, I use to think she was evil, had no sympathy in us I have learnt that she was a woman with a focus about the future of her off springs. Have you ever worked on a production line, my friend! It is not easy. You keep on asking to be moved from one point to the other, because you are not used to it. It is hard my friend it is not easy. You see the products coming from that side you have to put the top. When you see others working there, you might think you can, no ways my friend, no ways. Have you ever wet your bed be careful, you might. Some have mistaken their handbags for a toilet wet in there at night just because the handbag was white. Some have slept walking to work thinking it was in the morning they were suppose to go to work, whilst it's night time.

The weather here is different you cannot tell sometimes, so you need to use a watch. People are much disoriented to situations. E.g. confusion of days, dates place of work, due to working hard in so many places chasing after the pound. They confuse their work place go to a different place, and only to be told you are not booked. Thank god, the introduction of diaries assists a lot. Sometimes, I think there are many people who are now in a state of confusion, I hope it is not a disease. Fatigue is the norm of the day. What else can one do besides to sacrifice their life in order for the family at home survive?

Zimbabweans! Hello again, my friend hello! It is nice to hear that you are doing well. We had all the necessities of a day-to-day life on our hands. What did we do about it? Whilst others were busy trying to build Zimbabwe, others were busy with their five-pound hammers destroying it. It is like a caterpillar worms inside a maize cob, you know what I mean, and you will be made to think that, this year I will have a bumper harvest not knowing that someone inside hidden is doing a great job, eating very hard. What you will be left with is just an empty cob with nothing in it. Small country with great agricultural economic potential. Huh! Is it? Now they say small country with the worst chaos, lawlessness on earth, Corruption is the norm, no democracy, no respect of human rights that is Zimbabwe. I never heard of a country that cannot stand opposition. I use to think that if you have opposition in your parliament it will keep the ruling party on their feet trying very hard to put everything in order. The one it is more of eliminates the opposition. Now that you have many problems on hand, no doctors, no nurses, no professionals, most of them ran away, and decided to seek refuge in other countries. Where are you now, my friend, my motherland, Zimbabwe?

They long left for greener pastures, as proud people Zimbabweans they could not swallow their pride with the teargases thrown at them. When people expressed a political, or economic opinion by taking it to the streets, (demonstrations). Which is supposed to be a democratic thing in a democratic country, the riot police beat them for no apparent reason it was unbearable.

I thought I should rewind my memory back, take myself from the beginning of the War of the Rhodesian black people liberalization. As an observer from afar, I need to look, analyze things as they become clear in my mind, and elaborate them accordingly. It is important to elaborate; the information will be misinterpreted or lose its meaning. Right as from the 1960's there was a war of freedom, which was formed as Zimbabwe African Patriotic Union, which was organized by the people of origin, black people: Joshua Nkomo, Josiah Chinamano, Ndabaningi Sithole, Chitepo, Parirenyatwa, Silundika, Takawira, Zvobgo, Muzenda and the rest.

Well history explains itself, that black people organized mobilized a war that was against the oppression of the white minority rule of our country. The oppression became so obvious that people believe that this land belonged to the Majority, the black people of Zimbabwe. The black people of Rhodesia started to fight against the oppression, and human rights. There we comrades camp, which were set in our neighbouring countries, Mozambique, Zambia, Tanzania. In addition, other eastern European countries offered training for the freedom fighters, young people started running away from home to go to fight the black freedom war. They went and settled in the neighbouring countries, came in dodging the border posts and patrolling Rhodesian soldiers to fight the war for the black majority rule. There was an outcry sometimes when we use to here that the Rhodesian forces bombed the camps, and a number of youngsters perished. It was hard to think of it, because youngsters use to run away from home without telling their fathers and mothers that we are going to the war. Bless them, for what they did for the sake of freedom. However, one thing that has been hidden away from the people of Zimbabwe was that the atrocities of the war, the killings, and the disappearance of those who were, and those who are vocal about the governance never stopped although the war ended.

People fought a tough war; I mean a tough war. People perished in that tough war, they did perish! Young people who also wanted to enjoy the fruits of this country. I still, wonder what went wrong in the Promised Land, which was said to be full of honey and milk, the wishes of those who perished for the country, were they met, I don't know?

Black people of Zimbabwe never enjoyed democracy, never had freedom of speech or expressing what they want their country to do for them. It is a pity that it is only a few of us who can say it whilst we are out of the country, Zimbabwe.

The observer sometimes is a bit harsh on certain issues, because she was young and saw some of the political situations. Brothers and sisters, the observer, say she has a wound,

Which no one will heal because we have lost a beautiful country out of greediness and selfishness? Why is it that we want to be different from the rest of the world? What is so special about us, when in fact we cannot even afford to feed our own people? Why are we no more accommodative, were has the hospitalities gone, where had the love their neighbours gone? Why are people no more respecting the human nature?

The observer would like to ask a few questions to anyone who is prepared to answer him or her. Well, in all the truthfulness, kindness, in god's name, is that what people of Zimbabwe went to the war for? Why did we not just carryout a decree of understanding signed between the British government and the majority people of Zimbabwe that were against oppression and served bloodshed and lives of people? It is rather a painful thing for anyone who is observant as the observer herself.

This war brought many lies than the truth of the matter. The death of certain leaders was it timed or just unluckiness or a mystery that nobody will ever tell the people of Zimbabwe the truth of the matter. The country that people perished for is now a country of lawlessness, very poor, rather considered the poorest on earth. Corruption is more of a norm

Talk of instilling fear and intimidation. As this was experienced during the Rhodesian regime, why are black people suffering the same consequences in Zimbabwe this day and age? Firstly it was the Rhodesian government which instilled fear and intimidation to black people of Rhodesia then, now it is the Zimbabwean black government instilling fear and intimidation to its own people. I ask myself most of the time, did we break away from the past, or was the past better than the future? What is going on? Do not ask me I am as confused as you are. Mentally!

The observer is mostly observing these days or hallucinating about issues of the past and current affairs. What is now the outcome of the war? Animosity of people turning against one another. People live life by the day, price sky rocketing on a daily basis, inflation above 1,000,000%, and the Zimbabwean monetary currency has been changed several times. Political and economical problems in the country seem to be beyond control.

As an observer and a person of high integrity, I respect of myself I do believe that I am a human being moreover, bound to make mistakes just like anybody else. There are times I think I have a guardian angel, which leads my life, it guides me in certain ways, meaning I do have people trying to cone me just like at home. It sometimes makes me laugh. Foreigners in this country, England, you really surprise me, I am amazed by your cunning behaviour.

Can you imagine you came all the way from your country looking for greener pastures, now you start doing those pyramids, money clubs in a foreign land? You just make me sick in the head. Think, people think! What are you doing?

It made some our countries economy collapse; many people lost a lot of money. Tell me, that hard earning cash that you spend the whole night working for wiping bums or whatever. You think money grows on trees. Learn to work for everything nothing is free in this world. What you work sweat for is what you deserve. The observer sometimes become a fool for you, she is a woman of high integrity, respect human nature, because I cannot have money that I don't know where it is coming from, or neither can I cone my fellow country man for the sake of money. Heard that saying," Dull women have immaculate minds".

Well, I think I have been living in this other world of dreaming of things in a better way. The observer wants to talk about her country today, after observing from afar. I have seen women from my country today; they are not the women I think I use to know from home.

Women with great respect, women of high integrity, women of the soil, practically down to the earth, when it comes to be in public places. They now talk on top of their voices. They do not respect their surroundings. They talk of money care work nothing more. Let me tell you one thing, those who use to go to South Africa trading traditional goods are now here.

Well, I have been observing the current economic restructuring of the Zimbabwe; well it is like a joke, in anyway who wants to use banks more than the black market. Reluctantly, the black market is lucrative for the benefit of those who have the money already. However, the fact it is destroying the economy of the country. On the other hand, who are these people involved in the black market, big fish of course. That is the problem, which the observer from afar observes.

This day and age, abide by the rule, play it safe, you will never know who is who in the zoo. I have been observing from afar, trying to put myself in certain situations. Trying to think like other people in general, but alas, I did not want to be the other person, tried to be aimless, ignorant, carefree, not worrying about my country for a day, sorry I failed the test. I would rather be me, myself, I woman of adventure and very observant. Do as I wish, talk as I wish, write my lifetime revelations.

Have you ever sat down on your own and try to analyze things happening in the world nowadays. I do, because I have a good reason for it, maybe others also do, but they lack confidence in themselves. Are you still in denial as someone who can write something that annoys them, affects your moral, democratic rights that was robed from them? The world is supposed to be a habitable place. Nowadays we live in full of fear, intimidation and the future is unpredictable. I might sound like a wounded dog, or I have self-inflictor wounds. Maybe, I have seen the people that I emulated loved perish for no apparent reason.

Some might say there we go one's are now political. Well, take my word, if ever you think of other people in this whole world suffering the atrocities of war or in the hands of self-centred leaders, those who are power hungry like most African Leaders. I welcome you to the club because you are now a politician in every way.

Historically, or nowadays scientific or non-scientific research it requires two elements or two different components to achieve any results. Be it political or a socio-economic setup usually statistical figure to make comparison with and achieve results. Russians say, "Take three steps ahead, then take two steps backwards in order to achieve better results." Let me take explain myself fully, because it is not necessary for me to beat about the bush. You cannot be on your own in this world and think that you will manage. For the development of a country, we need each other from the North Pole to the South Pole. The world was created like that and the natural resources were laid the same, so that we could exchange and everyone could get what they can live on. We the people in the world are the two different elements or components. This is not happening because it is more like water and hot oil we cannot mix. Well, if ever I think of Zimbabwe, I see it as an accident, which was just waiting to happen. No one lives and works as a Solitary Island, we all influence other people in everything we do.

The observer wants to express herself about the farmers who were moved out of Zimbabwe. Do they have a birth right these people? South Africa managed to solve their racial problems by naming and shaming the people who were human rights violators and the mass killings of black people. Zimbabwe should have solved problems amicably, like the educated people, as we like to be seen on the international scenario. No matter how bad they were to the people of Zimbabwe and the damage they caused to people, the roundtable could have solved many problems rather than to moving them away from the farms. We do understand we needed land, but were we educated enough to take over, carry on as the previous commercial farmers.

As part of my observer ship I can take you, years back as to 1980. The aim of reconstruction of the Zimbabwean economy was equal opportunities to all. Which, I think it was going on well, before the regional status was put in place. During which I believe the international countries offered their help in educating Zimbabwean in every economic sector of the country. Then, creped in this thing called corruption, bureaucracy. It had to be a son of a relative of a minister or a minister's son or daughter to get a scholarship to study abroad, or any other financial assistance that maybe needed. It had to be from this region first. Whilst they were busy studying in Europe according to the five-year plans or ten-year plans, those without the right qualifications, already filled them, the posts as long as they were considered they were from the so-called region.

Let us go back to the more pressing issues, "farmers" on the other hand it was just a matter of having a round table talk with these farmers. They do have a right to be in that country Zimbabwe, as anybody else. If ever they had the problem of abusing their workers, as most of the workers were blacks that needed a very good addressing, and arresting not killing. The observer said you used your anger and became too emotional. Learn from South Africa, they lost their people but they let the people set a committee to sit down on a round table bring the culprit to justice, let them talk to the victim's relatives, see the pain they had caused, ask for forgiveness, from the families for those who were killed during their struggle. For us it seems its instant justice, which is wrong.

We need to strategise problem-solving strategies. The observer believes in carrying out feasibility study, in any situation. There was supposed to be laws for the necessities for the farm-workers in the hands of the white farmers. Those who failed to abide by the rule were supposed to have their farms taken given to others who had the knowledge of farming and believed in their workers services. That is what we call putting the mechanisms in place to accommodate everybody in the economy scenario of Zimbabwe.

Chapter 12

The observer is observing from afar, so who is who in Zimbabwe. You chased them instead of solving problems amicable. The farmers should have come to terms that they needed to share the fertile land with the majority of Zimbabweans, since the majority was settled in the barren land. Thank god some of the small land holders in the rural areas were working their way out managed to supply their fellow countrymen with fruits and vegetables just as good as white farmers. Nevertheless, the point was still that we needed the land to be redistributed. The majority has the fertile land to grow agricultural products for the society consumption, and the international Markey to boost our revenue for the development of our country, especially the much-needed foreign currency. Well, we cannot cry over spilled milk.

The farmers have relocated to your neighbours all over Africa. In some instances, they are offered to plough without paying any land rental for the next 90 years. Where are you now my friend? There is no hurry in Africa; do you know your enemies? Do you trust your neighbour to look after your wife? Look now they are laughing at you and say you are a fool. They have been longing to have what you had in Zimbabwe. They were busy admiring your wife whilst you were busy destroying your own economy. We thought they were behind you, when did they become truthful to you? We needed self-assessment my friend. It is like choosing friends, you need to choose them wisely, and we needed people who are constructive to be around you not the corrupt ones. Everything in this world you have to learn.

No one in this world was born a president, but you work your way to become one, the people of the sovereignty are the one is who chooses whom they wish. I definitely know it is a joke in other countries in Africa. It takes a lot to be a leader of people, or a father of a family. You just do not wake up one day you are a leader. The most truthful leaders are known for their love of their people they are never corrupt.

Well, I do not have to be negative on everything that happens to me most of the time. Let us look at the bright side of being in Europe. Well there are some instances that are good about being here in Europe, firstly and foremost the family will not starve, the kids will go to school, families at home can afford to have a meal each day. I think as a thinker, an observer I mean, I cannot resist thinking of those who were slow to react to the situation, as for when people started panicking about the economy showing signs of deteriorating, and they acted fast and left the country for greener pastures.

Well leaving the country has its own repercussions as well; it is not all that are going to catch the biggest worm. Some are here to accompany others. Heard that saying," You are an aimless person and you came to Europe because it was just a trend, since everybody was coming to Europe," take my word others came with something in mind. They wanted to learn make a change in their lives, they will achieve what they came for return home with something in their baskets, education, whilst others are just accompanying them. When it comes to education they will learn, Zimbabwean are education-orientated people they just like to get to know more. Moreover, others are just money orientated they do not believe in tomorrow. Education Zimbabweans will learn to their last drop of their blood. They read, they work, live in style.

As far as I can observe the educated Zimbabwean they believe in high class of life take my word they are people of high integrity, they respect other people are considered calm very highly qualified people. How can you tell that this Zimbabwean is coming from that other side of the world, I mean those who use to sell doilies in South Africa. Behaviour reflects itself the way they respond to situations. Very self centred always thinking of themselves. They are not having the togetherness that destroyed our country. If you work with them, for example, when duties are being allocated they want the most, because they are mostly focused on making money. They do not think of developing themselves education wise, they do not have this tomorrow at the back of their mind.

I have observed one woman who is very dark talks about herself and the so-called highly qualified husband, whom she portrait as heaven and earth for her, he earns more than anybody else does in this country. I mean foreigners, I suppose.

When I look at her, I see an uneducated woman who is a gold digger by marrying this rich man. Well, what amazed me is she should not have been wiping bums then, just like anybody else, whom is not proud of themselves, they get on with their work support their families at home and for that matter, they do not gossip about anything. This woman is as ugly as I cannot explain as black as a miner can be from the underground shift, before they take a shower. When she smiles, you would think she is crying. That is just ugly. These Zimbabwean are greedy and they can do anything to get money, sell their bodies, work until they drop, they do anything to get the so-called pound. Moreover, if only they could sell a pound of flesh, I bet they would, as long as they can lay their hands on the money. In addition, their conversations they talk about money, exchange rate, how to scrutinize papers to get another job and earn more money, low tax rates. In my life I have come across people who love money but his group of people I raise my hands I rest my case!

Oh! Well, I have been observing the wrong side of my story in a way. I want to be more specific now about these international people from all occupations, these people are displaced by economic hardships of their countries. Some are here they did not intend to be here, but the situation forced them to be in this situation. Let us look at people who came here to make ends meet. They work hard, they help their families with money they earn, they go to college to upgrade themselves, learning new careers and expect to go back home one day and be the highly qualified person from Europe. On the other hand, some other people are here to talk about their businesses at home. In addition, they praise themselves on how many trucks they have send home how much money they are making out of their trucks. However, after a few hours they start running around borrowing some money for paying rent, or for buying food, for even buying fuel for their cars.

There is nothing like living comfortable out of their earnings, but it is more of they can sleep under the bridge as long as they can save money. Some die of fatigue, some go mad. I cannot believe these people; this thing off coming to Europe has managed to bring out the true reflection of people of Zimbabwe and their classes. They want if they can try to live on others expense. They sleep here today tomorrow there. They criticize everything from their work place to the person who assisted them, when they came to Europe. At the end of the day, they do not see eye to eye with the relatives who have been their stepping-stones for their survival. The moment they secure a job, settled in a small room, they forget about their relations.

Others it is different because it depends on the situation you are in. some they want you to pay for the help they gave you, for the rest of your stay here in Europe. That is disgusting! You help, it is your wish and that is the end of the story.

Now I have a new name that I decided to give myself, instead of observer, I think I prefer to be an on-lookers type of person and I want to try to meditate or sort of daydream. I want to be a forecaster now. I have not been in such a good mood these days due to pressure of work and homesickness. In any case, I have not stopped to look and listen. Now that people are moving from one point to the other, and working in different towns, relocation, relocation, relocation there isn't much to write about, besides for those ones who stay at one place for years because these are no worries type of people and they take it easy, that is me, lay back type of person.

Well, I have a day off today; I decided to do a bit of shopping for my toiletries and a bit of groceries, just like my fellow citizens of this country that is offering me shelter at this given time. One thing that I will always remember is the British people are shopper holics, they buy and sometimes I wonder why they shop like that. In this country, they shop every weekend the town centres are always packed with people shopping. As compared to home, people use to do serious groceries only once a month, even clothes, people use to buy, as and when they have buying power on their accounts in the departmental shops. However, here it is an ongoing process. Well as for some of us from abroad, we are here for a different reason.

Chapter 13

Zimbabwe my country, historical issues when I look at the International countries, and also looking at the British settlers who settled in Zimbabwe. Were they wrong to come and settle in our country, Zimbabwe? This question sometimes puzzles me I think those who came did get the best of the fertile land, lived well, they forgot the majority of the people, or rather, they were carried away and forgot that they will be a wakeup call one day was wrong. How was this issue supposed to be solved? I think it needed to be addressed in a more professional way. Then I assume that the International countries cannot comment on an action taken by the Zimbabwean government on farm invasion was right because there has never been a comment on this issue.

As for the war, which was fought in Zimbabwe, was based on the reclamation of the ancestral land. Africa can solve its own problems. I do not think so, No, it is creeping into Europe slowly. The African problems are world problems as far as I am concerned. We live in this world together, what I am saying is, this is a take it or leave it situation, huh! I do not know, I suppose it makes sense in a way. You get what I mean. Love thy neighbour. Because if you look at the migration of Africans to Europe that own its own shows that Africa needs help, I think someone somewhere should put themselves in the shoes of a migrant person for a day. These men, women they leave their wives, children in their countries of origin, come to Europe to do what the people of Zimbabwe call (BBC) British Bottom Cleaning. It is not an insult to these people; it is the survival of the fittest. They do the dirtiest jobs you can think of, I am not complaining but I need this to be known that there is a very good reason for this. We are the former grandchildren of the former British colony. This is a survival of the fittest and those who managed to catch the freedom train. I believe through hardship one day we will get there.

Land redistribution in Zimbabwe, needed addressing in a very serious way. Well from the beginning, it was a very sad situation because they displaced Zimbabweans and made them settle on barren land. They struggled to grow food for their consumption, but they ended up failing to produce enough for their needs and end up working at close by commercial farm owned by a British settler. The set up for the Tribal Trust Lands near a commercial farm would advantage a white man in the context that cheap labour was provided. Because these black people who lived in the villages nearby the commercial, farms were bound to go and work at this farm in order to sustain their families. This was due to poverty. Their children would attend a school, which was strategically build in the farm, and the parents will be working in the fields, and the parents had a stop order, which was offered by the farm owner, in order to pay for their children's education.

The parents practically worked for nothing because they were offered a credit system that they always owed the farmer. They were given ration food from the farmer every week that is a bucket of maize meal, and half bucket of beans, since maize meal is the main meal for Zimbabwean. This set up was a disadvantage to the workers, they never had money in their pockets, I mean part of their earnings go to clear a credit for the children's school fess, and the other for groceries which were borrowed at a small convenient shop which was build by the farmer and owned by the farmer.

Every month these men and women their take home was absolutely nothing. They had clothes like uniform because they had a society of their own, the tailor who worked for the farmer sowed their clothes and fashion was a story tale. They had this outstanding dressing code, which quickly identified them from the rest of the people. I do remember seeing some of them with these summer dresses, which had gathers on the waist or box plaits. The colourful printed materials were colour blinding, and lasted only one wash. It was just that cheap material from the Indian shops down the town, Salisbury then now Harare. Their form of entertainment was based on the farmer's mood, that is over the weekend, when the workers were given a day off. The farmer would play his record player, they had this type of music that I do not think, I have ever heard it played in Harare, were I was born. It was weird. It was our own it was sung by the new imaging farm worker singers. However, it usually ended up there. As far as redistribution of land was concerned, it was long overdue. We definitely needed to learn to live together and the original people of Zimbabwe needed to be resettled.

The equal opportunity rights mechanism in place and stop slave labouring. It is quite an emotional issue when you think of it; it gives you a lump on your throat and a chilling fever. That is if you are human enough. It was an issue, which needed addressing in an amicable way, rather than hoping and jumping into conclusion. I do feel for anybody who is a Zimbabwean and who can be a thinker, just like me, can understand.

On the other hand, this issue was blown out of proportion by being implemented at the wrong time, the timing was not right at all, it was not supposed to be used as a political weapon, since a lot of the International countries saw it that way. The political situation in Zimbabwe has taken many turns, the introduction of the opposition, and the falling down of the country's economy. Corruption, everyday you would read about someone has done this, swindling the government funds.

The Zimbabwean government was much more involved in the monetary issues of the local government of its major towns. That resulted in the failure of proper functioning of the well-being of people. Although there was a residential parliament representative, everything seems to have been controlled from the Zimbabwean parliament, instead of the people and the representative, and their areas of dwelling. Things took a wrong twist. Funds accumulated from the services offered by the council, disappeared, the residents were no more receiving the services they need, e.g. garbage is not collected, busted water pipe not being repaired, and sewage pipes bust and stay a week or more without being repaired.

The people of Zimbabwe started getting disillusioned by the government, during the referendum, they did not vote for the current government, but the government's mechanism was in place, so much that the voice of the people was not heard, or it was ignored. According to certain sources, the president was told that people no more want you, they want you to go. Nevertheless, he insisted on staying, and replied they are going to like, and I will make them like me. Whatever happened, to this country called Zimbabwe? I just do not know, because when you hear the so-called first world talking about Zimbabwe you will think there something in store for poor Zimbabweans. Well it is heart breaking to hear nothing at the end of the day.

Well the thing is, this is genocide at its best this Zimbabwean government is just killing people psychologically. All these issues need to be addressed in favour of the people of Zimbabwe.

I do agree that you cannot just build your house anywhere you feel like, it really needs planning and the town planning infrastructure had already fallen apart. It is easier said than done. Planning in Zimbabwe is just harp hazard. It seems everything is based on political challenges, now people feel it is because people of Zimbabwe living in towns voted for the

opposition is the main reason why there was this destruction of their houses, and relocation of people. The whole world is watching and comments we are so tired of them, we need action and help. Bad timing again the Zimbabwean government has done it again.

Well the clean up was long overdue, especially the towns not the urban area particularly. Because the town was no better looked after? Why, because of the town council setup. There are certain townships like for instance Mbare. This township has been breeding many of the thieves; people were just living by the bus stop. People are meant to be resettled in a human nature way, not to be treated like animals. That is where many people differ with the government. They make promises today, later they are taking a twist. People are treated like animals.

Transferring people from one point to the other needs a lot of infrastructure planning. In this case, people are just being thrown in the bush. Just like dumping a dog or any animal for no apparent reason. Most of the issues that arise in Zimbabwe are nerve raking. Why should the international world who denied that there is no aids' exist in Africa whilst people were dying every day? Talk of people living like rats, in Africa people live in shacks made out of barrel metal drums being cut straightened make a home. Therefore, when you talk of brick houses they do not understand what you are talking of.

We do agree so much on the clean up, the thing that we disagree to these issues is the time factor that these setting up take place. People need to be considered, talked to give them time to move on. I wonder, is this the government that people voted for, a one-man band, or a few of those other people. People of Zimbabwe need to solve their own problems with many help from the international. What I mean is, by getting out of that country is enough to demonstrate that we are against the political, economical status in Zimbabwe.

I cannot believe it; Zimbabwe's shunt houses sounds as if it is the first one on this earth to have such accommodation. Yes, we must admit these houses do house thieves that are not proper for people to live in those houses. The question remains, people are already suffering, why add some more problems to them. Why is it that anything that is carried out in Zimbabwe, I mean any government decisions just take a split second people are being harassed? Why is it that there is no human respect? These same people vote for this government. No, wonder why people are disillusioned. People use to think there is a light at the end of the tunnel, now people live by the day. No fuel, basic commodities prizes out of reach, no democracy. I definitely wonder whether the President of Zimbabwe goes to bed, sleep whilst the nation sleeps in the open air, with their future people of Zimbabwe, young children. I sometimes fail to swallow my mouth runs dry, I feel a lump in my throat, each time I see on the television how the people of Zimbabwe are suffering. Are these the people you expect to vote for you all the times the elections are run?

Time heals all wounds; he who laughs last, laughs the longest. I will abide my great lump fresh to see your product out of this. Therefore, many people had all the respect for Zimbabwe it is not easy to talk, but time will tell.

No one is against the resettling of people it is true that the towns were not what they use to be. We were known of the cleanliness of our major towns the whole set up was good. We did lay back a bit the migration of people from the rural areas was not very good. People were just settling for the big cities, bright lights. However, to be quite honest, there were a lot of development in the rural areas that included the introduction of solar panels, introduction of gas, using cow dung, people in the rural areas could see televisions, and gas cookers were introduced.

Let us look at our Zimbabwean issue today, Zimbabwe, "CLEAN-UP". What is this clean up and to what extent? This is the problem; there is no consultation with the people of Zimbabwe that voted for the Black Zimbabwean majority rule. Why it is that now it is a one-man band? Why is it that the settling infrastructure is carried out just like that before hand? In any case, I think you cannot just dump people in a forest expect them to survive. Why is it that the government did not build houses first, and then settle people? The reason being, yes! People in towns did not vote for them because they want fresh blood to help with running of the country after many economy failures.

The development of the country Zimbabwe was all thrown through a window. The socio-economic of Zimbabwe was forgotten, instead of thinking about how to develop our industrial and agricultural sectors and put aside politics. Everything took a wrong turn. Politics became the norm. There was nothing as if how can we learn to have enough food reserves for those dry years. How can we try to follow those new ways that those in deserts are trying to ploughing in dry lands? We were busy fighting against one another. Tribalism, what is tribalism in the world.

Do we sit down and think of the children that we are bringing into this world under these circumstances. Hatred! For what reason? I think some people were just born evil, and I find it very hard to follow. If ever was a chosen to be a leader, the truth of the matter shows in their doings.

The importance of bringing human rights violators to justice was that it clearly demonstrated that it was a declaration that no one is above the law, including those even the most powerful members of the state apparatus. For this reason, the obligation on the authorities to bring charges against those believed to have committed human rights abuse is even greater than when similar crimes are committed by ordinary citizens. Unfortunately, by

means of indemnity regulations, amnesties and simple failure to prosecute, the Zimbabwean government has instead created the impression that certain agencies – notably the CIO, but on occasions branches of the police and army too – are a law unto themselves. The retention of torturers and other human rights violators in positions of authority and the failure to take action against them unmistakably suggest that the government does not regard such crimes as serious. They also greatly increase the likelihood that human rights violations will recur. The government's failure to take action against human rights violators also discourages individuals from complaining about abuses for fear that they will be further victimized.

The Zimbabwean Government has been criticized for failing to amnesty civilians imprisoned for "dissidents" offences, when it has released members of security forces who have committed similar or often more serious, crimes. This inconsistency reinforces the impression that members of the security forces and ruling party are not subject to the rule of law.

Africa Watch urges the government to release all those serving sentences for "dissidents" offences under a general amnesty. They also urge that there be no future general amnesties for those responsible for human rights abuses and the government's intention to prosecute those of its servants who abuse human rights be clear and publicized for the people of Zimbabwe.

Africa Watch also urges the government to repeal the protection of Wildlife (Indemnity) Act, passed earlier that year, which protects game wardens from prosecution for abuses. They consider that this was likely to encourage such abuses as well as being contrary to the basic principle of equality before the law.

Payment of compensation was one of the most important remedies when agents of the state violate an individual's rights. The right to seek redress through courts is guaranteed in international human rights instruments. Yet, despite several rulings by Zimbabwean courts in favour of victims of abuse, the government has apparently never paid compensation

Africa Watch urged the Zimbabwean government to alter its practice in this regard and to make compensation payments to victims of human rights abuse, including unlawful detention and torture, as well as to the relatives of people who have "disappeared" or been victims of political killings by members of the security forces. Such payments should be made without prejudice to any other criminal or civil proceedings.

A precondition to both the prosecution of human rights violators and the payment of compensation to those whose rights have been abused is the prompt and impartial investigation of allegations of abuse. Under its Commissions of Inquiry Act Zimbabwe has the mechanism to conduct major investigations with most of the necessary guarantees of impartiality. Its major weakness is that it does not require investigations to be conducted publicly or to publish their conclusion. Thus, for example, a major commission of inquiry on human rights abuses in Matebeleland in 1983 reported to the government but its findings have never been made public. Although human rights investigations may occasionally have to proceed in private, the general rule should be that they are public in order to safeguard their impartiality.

There are two issues in particular still need inquiry. One is the unresolved question of "disappearances," both of prisoners held in police custody and of people abducted in rural areas of Matebeleland and Midlands, apparently by the security forces. The aim of such investigations would be to determine their whereabouts, to enable death certificates to be issued where appropriate, to facilitate the payment of compensation to their relatives and to prepare for criminal prosecution of those responsible for the "disappearances."

The second issue, which needs investigation, is the continuing use of torture, particularly by the CIO. The aim of such an investigation would be to establish the truth of continuing allegations of torture, to facilitate the payment of compensation to those who have been tortured and to prepare criminal prosecutions of those law enforcement officials alleged to have carried out torture. Pending criminal proceedings, they should be removed from their posts.

In addition, there should be a permanent mechanism whereby individual complaints of abuse can be investigated. By this means, a person who alleges that he or she has been tortured or that a relative has "disappeared" can have his or her complaint promptly impartially investigated.

This might be achieved, by expanding the existing office of the ombudsman, who looks into complaints of maladministration. However, such a body should also have discretion to initiate inquiries when there has been no complaint, since there are many reasons why people who have suffered traumatic experiences such as torture may be reluctant to come forward to present their complaint.

Although it ratified the African Charter on Human and People's Rights in 1986, Zimbabwe is not part of any of the major United Nations human rights instruments. Africa Watch urges the Zimbabwean Government to begin moves to ratify the International Covenant on Civil and Political Rights (with its Optional Protocol) and the Convention Against Torture or Other Cruel, Inhuman or Degrading Treatment or Punishment. Not only do these treaties give legal force to the human rights first codified in the Universal Declaration of Human Rights (of which the Zimbabwean Government has declared itself a staunch supporter); they also incorporate mechanisms for reviewing the adherence of states to the provisions of the treaties and investigating complaints from individuals who claim that their rights have been violated.

Chapter 14

Zimbabwe's economic status showed its cracks when some of the government senior staff started helping themselves with the government monies, basically the people's monies. This issue of the economy going down started soon after the introduction of the Economic Structural Adjustment Programme (ESAP), which was introduced by the International countries. This ESAP did not help Zimbabwe at all; actually, it destroyed the economy, instead of building it. It became a loophole for those who were on the upper hand of the projects, which were being implemented.

They were reports of projects being carried out in the development of the rural areas and the infrastructure of the towns, but alas, that was a joke the funds were untraceable. Then there was the borrowing of funding from the IMF. What is IMF in Africa? It is a profit making organization, which borrows African countries money at a high interest rate, which you will never finish paying for the rest of your life. The poorest countries in Africa give back more in debt repayments than they get in Aid.

Debt is enslaving the world's poorest people. In Africa, we did not live on credit. In Europe, you will come to realize that people live on credit cards. They introduced this borrowing in Africa, and countries started borrowing not knowing the consequences of this until they were in such debt that they failed to pay back. Are you with me so far, because sometimes, I do not know what I want to say since I am a person of so many words? I sometimes even chew my tongue, because words rather tongue-tied my words that cannot wait to get out of my mouth..

Whilst the people of Zimbabwe believed that nature provided their needs, not their greed. The only thing that really changed was the way people started being greedy wanting more than what they were capable of getting. The opening up of the boarders, allowed people to travel sees what was outside Zimbabwe. I am not saying that was bad but it brought back a lot of trade which the government did not get any import duties for or rather managed to get any revenue to boast the economy.

On the other hand, if only during this process when people started wanting products from outside Zimbabwe, designer clothes, the government should have used companies that were registered for importing in order to get the import duties revenue, which was government stipulated, and to observe the trading of the companies, rather than to let anyone travel to anywhere in the world and bring whatever they want, sell at exorbitant prices no duty paid due to bribing the customs officer, who is also disillusioned by the pay check he or she gets every month. This was not easy; people had to survive one way or the other. Still, the government laid back a lot that is why we have many problems in Zimbabwe. In addition, I suppose some of the people who were trading were family members of the ministers. *Now that we want to go back to the drawing board start all over again. It makes me laugh, but as a Zimbabwean, I still hope for the best, because if I give up who will stand up for me?*

On the other hand, Africans emulate the first world and think that we are, as Africans should live like the first world. There are people like Julius Nyerere who led his country in poverty according to the first world standards, of which I think that man was right. Look at the world events talk of simple invasion of other countries on this earth.

These countries were created with natural resources. They belong to the native people of those countries. This is the problem lies, invasion of other countries. Usually, if you are in your normal faculties, you would ask yourself, why are you here? Because this will solve many questions, life wise. Firstly, we say we came to seek refugee from the atrocities of our country, but reality is we are economic refugees some of us because of not managing to afford basic commodities in our countries. Some people believe that they are asylum seekers; some are economic refugees, running away from poverty and starvation. Home is always great, there is no place like home. On the other hand, they need to be here for the survival of their family members they left home, in Africa.

Migration is a natural movement for people in political or economical situations when people start failing to provide for their families and feeling air beneath their feet. General because we have Bushmen, in Africa, when the weather is cold; they travel to the areas nearer the equator where it is a bit warmer during the southern of Africa winters. Historically, people use to migrate when the soil is no more fertile, and the weather as well was a common factor. Migration of today is based upon political and economical hardships. The difference is the borders, which limits people's migration.

Think of before civilization when the world was just one piece, then you can imagine how it was like. I think people use to have a common language they were not greedy as we are today. I have seen it witnessed, that there is respect of thy neighbour. We are now money oriented we can sell, or neither kills for the sake of money. What is not sold in this world from toddles to adults, sex, land, food, natural resources materials?

Africa needs to integrate big time, because when you look at the resources that are in Africa, naturally we can trade amongst ourselves without first selling goods to the first world. Look at China today; they are dominating in the industrial production. In Africa, we need to have trust be dedicated to our people. Trust truthfulness is the only factor that can help build Africa. Talk of leaders who are power hungry these people should try to figure out how to run their countries according to our African chief man ship, that will solve many problems than the election selected presidents and prime ministers.

If you look at how a simple man in the streets in Africa how they strive work hard to support their political leaders, you will just be amazed as to why do they do that, how their leaders turn back against their own people after some years in power. Why is it that they end up being the multi millionaires defrauding government's monies, that is suppose to enable to run the country. Those monies belong to the people; will end up belonging to one or two people.

Why it is that people turn to corruption, become murderers, and power hungry after all? At the end of the day, they are not happy because their conscience will be killing them inside. They do not know that, "the secret of being miserable is to have enough leisure to wonder if you are happy". Remember no one lives and works as Solitary Island, we all influence other people in everything we do. At the end of the day one would like to look back, be proud of their achievements. I just wonder, but at least, I can look back and say I wrote these revelations for the future generation of Zimbabwe and the world to know the truth. The best part of it I have researched the truth of some of the atrocities, which were never published in Zimbabwe.

Chapter 15

Recapture of economic events, my experiences take me back when Rhodesia (then Zimbabwe) was a country, which was habitable the international fraternity emulated the country. They called it the jewel of Africa, the breadbasket of the southern Africa. Zimbabwe produced food for its surrounding neighbouring countries, exchanged products with its neighbours sold agricultural products on the international markets. Whereby neighbourhood, friendship was sealed with agricultural shows, which was a pride of Zimbabwe, showing off, what we were capable of producing, all the agricultural latest equipment and produce.

The famous Harare Agricultural Show was an event not to miss every year in August. The best farmers and production companies, in any sector were rewarded with gifts, for their good work in development of technology, the latest companies in the industry and their products. The best farmer for animal breeds, horse show jumping's, Eh! Gone are the days, you can imagine, how I feel. We had a life. We once supplied agricultural produce for its neighbouring countries, exchanged products with its neighbours. This was ruled out as good neighbouring. Exportation of agricultural produce flourished, especially horticultural produce, we did well on the international market.

After the country got back to black Africans, it was welcomed with open arms. The excitement was overwhelming if you looked into people's eyes you could see the glow in their eyes this was exciting. At last, we have a black majority rule in Zimbabwe and everybody is free, democracy has finally knocked on African people of Zimbabwe household doors.

All other countries in Africa, the international fraternity send their congratulations. Some were invited to the state banquet for the inauguration of the black majority independence. The British were given back their union jack flag, of which Lord Somme's and Prince Charles attended. We had all that we wanted. We would go to placed that we were not allowed and we had the jobs that we never dreamed of having. So where did we go wrong? Why is it that we are now rated the poorest in the whole world? I will try to put you in picture later but firstly let me put you clarify a few issues.

We had, in Zimbabwe the non-governmental organization coming in to help us develop set up the country's infrastructure, following the rural cultural based system that we had. We had pit toilets build and they were very hygienic we had boreholes sunken; people had clean water for their household use. The non-governmental organizations came up with the introduction of using cow dung to create a gas for the rural use, instead of cutting down the trees. This was a way of trying to preserve the rural natural resources. The rural population understood the natural conservation of trees and the fact that they gave them fresh air.

There was also an introduction of a rural based health care assistant who was send for training on basic first aid, medication administering, say for headaches, malaria, and diarrhoea, and other tropical diseases some of them were usually the midwifery woman for the village, they worked hand in hand with the elderly woman for assistance in giving birth, in accordance with our cultural values. Everything was hunky dory that time. We enjoyed going to the Tribal Trust Lands because we could watch television due to the introduction of solar panels.

This all came into play due to the introduction of latest technologies to the Tribal Trust Lands for the people. The development was based on people, to the people. Because people of Zimbabwe helped to fight for black majority rule, then they should get the best out of it. People were happy that the war was over we learned to live together with the white minority just flow with the independence, but some was not for it, they left the country, but those who remained, with time they understood that we need to live together and compromise one another. The best preparation for the uncertain tomorrow is the fulfilment of the certain today.

How was this issue of land supposed to be solved? I think it needed to be addressed in a more professional way. Then, I assume that the International countries cannot comment on an action taken by the Zimbabwean government on farm invasion was right because there has never been a comment on this issue.

Did they take the land without permission, or was there an agreement between the British government the Zimbabwean government, that failed to materialize, because as for the war which was fought is Zimbabwe is the reclamation of the ancestor land. There was no two ways about that. Well it was a very sad situation because they displaced Zimbabweans made them settle on barren land. They struggled to grow food for their consumption they ended up failing to produce enough for their household needs end up working at close by commercial farm owned by a British settler. There seem to be lack of transparency in issues like this, which involve the movement of people.

The set up for Tribal Trust Lands near a commercial farm would advantage a white man in the context that cheap labour was provided. Because these Zimbabweans nearby the commercial farms were bound to go work at this farm in, order to sustain their families. Their children would attend a school, which was strategically build in the farm, the parents will be working in the fields, the parents had a stop order, which was offered by the farm owner, in order to pay for their children's education. The parents practically worked for nothing because they were offered a credit system that they always owed the farmer. They were given ration food from the farmer every week that is a bucket of maize meal, half bucket of beans, since maize meal is the main meal for Zimbabwean.

This set up of Tribal Trust lands was a disadvantage to the black workers, they never had money in their pockets, I mean part of their earnings go to clear a credit for the children's school fees, the other for groceries which were borrowed at a small convenient shop which was build by the farmer owned by the farmer. Every month these men and women their take home was absolutely nothing. They had clothes like uniform because they had a society of their own, the tailor who worked for the farmer sowed their clothes and fashion was a story tale. They had this outstanding clothing system. I do remember seeing some of them with these summer dresses, which had gathers on the waist or box plaits. The colourful materials which were sown were colour blinding. It was just that cheap material from the Indian shops down the town, that was Salisbury then, now Harare. As far as redistribution of land was concerned, it was long over due. Don't you wonder what was the government busy doing if it was what we fought for?

We definitely needed to learn to live together the black people of Zimbabwe needed to be resettled, get the equal rights mechanism in place and stop slave labouring. It is quite an emotional issue when you think of it; it gives you a lump on your throat and a chilling fever. That is if you are human enough. It was an issue, which needed addressing in an amicable way, rather than hopping and jumping into conclusion. I do feel for anybody who is a Zimbabwean can be a thinker, just like me. It takes a lot to think like this to reach this point, a point of no return in life. Being a beggar in another country is not easy. For that matter being somewhere where you are not wanted is even worse your downfall brings the whole family down. However, what else can one do, besides to hope for the best. You live in fear of the unknown and uncertainty.

There were people like Eric Block, the economist, I respect the man who had already established a good relationship with blacks he had no problems to interact with fellow Zimbabweans. He was the presenter of the High School's quiz, which was sponsored by Old Mutual Insurance Company. You would not want to miss such television programmes, which were very educative and informative for those still going to school and promoting education. It helped many schools to do better. Moreover, pupils wanted to study hard to put their school on top of every High School in Zimbabwe. People like Simon Parkinson the DJ; work for him was just as usual.

We had it all, my friends we had it in the land of honey and milk, Zimbabwe motherland. He had a lot on his radio programmes that most Zimbabweans would not miss for the world. There came our own Zimbabwean James Maridhadhi was the nations favourite, he was very popular with the kids. He use to do a kids radio programme, after Mbuya Chirambakusakara retired. He was a hero to every four to seven year old, who would phone in and request their special music to be played.

On television, the Zimbabwean Broadcasting Corporation we had many African dramas, which were acted, following the actual living way of our Zimbabwean family setup and some had a lot of humour that you would laugh your lungs out. Musically we were kept in touch with the international music by John Matinde that was on television every Saturday evening, "Sounds on Saturday". This kept many kids off the streets and out of mischief and bad behaviour. The British call that time family time together.

I remember that we use to have our supper early on Saturday, and do the wash up and clean the kitchen and prepare soft drinks to drink and pop corn to eat whilst we watched the Saturday family favourite programmes. We had a life in Zimbabwe and life was just moving on smoothly. All we have to do now is to look back and reflect and with a bit of a tear shed, you just say I hope that one day we will get there.

No one make you inferior without your consent. We are the making of this government, I do not know how other people of Zimbabwe feel because, we were used for the suffering of our brothers and sisters, we were robbed our freedom to enjoy the Mother Nature fruits of Zimbabwe. I feel we were used as a ritual sacrifice for the benefit of the others. If only we were sacrificed for something better I would not be here and feeling as guilt as I feel right now. In any case, we are pigs roasted themselves in their own fat.

Everybody who walks on earth has an excuse for their behaviour. There is continual shifting of balance between good and bad within each of us and in the external world. What is scary is that, now, bad winning. There is a sense of despair in the world.

News footage of terrible wars, violence, crime, the horrors of disease and famine, all the global catastrophes, as long as these things do not touch our personal lives, we do not care. Most people are caught up in their own lives and their own problems. We dissociate ourselves from pain, strife, and the lives of others. I think in times gone past, we needed each other more. Helping each other was a more normal and instinctive way of life. These days, we view other people's problems as their own. It is easy to think in simplistic terms of someone being a bad person, and a nun being a good person, but these are just extremes. All actions in between the ordinary mundane ones count as well". "We are all accountable for the choices that we make. However, nobody and no action are beyond redemption. The difference between someone who has strayed down the wrong path and someone who is truly evil is that evil has no sense of remorse, never feels sorry.

Zimbabweans are now scattered all over the world and some even saying I will never go back to Zimbabwe again. However, I believe in my sixth sense, that you are not supposed to say never in your life. I do not think that is practical, anyone who came here, to Europe was hoping to spend much time; I bet it was specifically for a short time. In other instances to just work and get enough money to live on, in a short space of time. This was due to people not affording the necessities of everyday needs. But, alas, as the economy of Zimbabwe started going down, a lot of people including myself had the high hopes, and believed it shall come to pass as soon as they is an understanding. A miracle that is what everybody hoped for.

Moreover, since some of us we were born during the Rhodesian period, I suppose we have the same life styles then.

Now comes that time again we are over five to seven years in England. We are supporting our families at home and we are able to buy those things, which were out of reach for some of us. We definitely believe we will get there one day, if ever comes up with a solution to resolve the problems of the economy of Zimbabwe and the political status and be able to pay all the country's debts. I do consider that we are the unsung hero's in this country because there isn't very much being talked about us, we work very hard and we do the dirty work that I think some of you people will never attempt to do.

Zimbabwe's economy was and is naturally based on agricultural production and mining. I use to enjoy watching the Zimbabwe Broadcasting Corporation when they use to announce the Gross Domestic Products (GDP) exports, how much tobacco was sold out, and how much foreign currency have been acquired to boost our ever growing economy. It was a pleasure to see and appreciate that the farmers were doing a great job in order to keep the economy of the country stable and sustainable for the people of Zimbabwe.

We were there when the prominent black business people started to buy businesses the tobacco floors, which where build by the famous prominent people of Zimbabwe and we could see the sales on television. It was uplifting to see a black man owning big companies. There were quite a number of black prominent businesspersons and women who were doing well in the development of new businesses or taking over from a white Zimbabwean who could not stand the black majority rule. It was a dream come true for others, and commiserations for others. However, I suppose, I reserved my comment during that time due to my sixth sense, which kept me thinking as a thinker. I did not vote during that time because of my consciences.

I remember I went to the places where people were voting, because my mother said I should go and vote, I did but when I was in the queue I changed my mind and turned and walked back home and told my mother I had voted. It is amazing, how I have managed to keep this secret for twenty-six years. If ever she is going to find out she will wonder but she would not be surprised. The thing is I did not trust what was going on I suppose.

The fact that I had a cousin, (the late) who came back from the war, and the teaching that they had learned there did put me off. Why? Because it was like holiday everyday and there was nothing like serious thinking and organizing their life besides believing that they were going to be staying in the white owned houses, and other political concepts that were so unbecoming. He never believed that he needed to work harder than before to help develop our country.

It was a pity, until one day when I stopped him and told him we have had enough of the party slogans, he feared me so much because he once picked a fight with me, when I was seventeen years old and I beat the hell out of him I really showed him what I was. He respected me so much from that day. I did beat the hell out of a boy that is what my mother use to say, you are a strong girl, out of my stomach came out a strong girl!

On the other hand, Zimbabwe's major towns are divided, just like the Berlin wall east and west, the other side people are throwing food away, the other side people are suffering unemployed and very, very poor. Now the economic setup has separated people. A good example is going to Sam Levy's in Borrowdale. Those in uptown suburban areas who are not starving at all, and if you talk of starvation they look at you as if you have a problem with the political setup of Zimbabwe, more than just being a concerned citizen of Zimbabwe with an open-mind about their surroundings. Just a caring person about the welfare of your fellow citizens of Zimbabwe the one is who put this government in power, now they are looked down upon as political problems to the sovereignty of Zimbabwe.

Conclusion

You are going to realise that I have written this book in general, some other issues I have personalised them, due to being emotional to certain events that I think they were misleading to the people of Zimbabwe. Reading has also helped me to research a lot about the government of Zimbabwe, which was supposed to look after its own people, give the rightful security. Nevertheless, the Zimbabwean government is the one, which has a high rate in violation of human rights. I am emotional to a number of issues, situations like why they let people, the people of the Zimbabwe, the so-called sovereignty of Zimbabwe built houses first, and then destroy their houses. I think people understand an infrastructure of a town, because they know how towns are set up, the water, the sewage systems, moreover how it works.

Most of these issues are used as political instruments to annoy and morally destroy the people's human rights and lives were lost in this process. Politically correctness is an issue; it is overpowered against people's rights. They were not supposed to let them built, **period!** It is just like oh! Oh! The government has done it again wrong timing. People were sold this land and others were allocated according to the city of Harare. It is more like Zimbabwe is for the people as and when they are in good books with the government. If you look at Harare, it has long been years having plans of growing into a bigger town. The water and sewage systems were already in for expansion. They were supposed to be allowed to do what they wanted, but the reality of the situation is in the creation of accommodation for all. I still remember the railway line, which was planned to be laid from Harare town centre to Chitungwiza. Where did that government plan go? There were many plans for the towns. However, people of Zimbabwe never asked or voiced their concerns, and then the Zimbabwe government dooms their wishes.

Firstly, this was my diary, which I was writing how I felt, everyday events, especially the political and economical situation in Zimbabwe. However, due to many people who encouraged me to put it in writing and all the library staff who never got tired of my requests. Some of them did not know this country. I had to research some of the material that I used to write this book. My country Zimbabwe, my views, how I feel, became interesting to listen to, they thought it would be a revelation to other people who do not know about my country called Zimbabwe and those who were born in Zimbabwe, the so called born free. I hope everybody who is going to read this book will enjoy it. I hope it will change your views, your assumptions of our country Zimbabwe. To all disillusioned people of the sovereignty of Zimbabwe, heard that saying," Him to be, whatever your labours and aspirations, in the noisy confusion of life keep peace with your soul. With all its sham, drudgery and broken dreams it is still a beautiful world". Be careful. Strive to be happy, respect human nature, let us live, love one another.

Just think of it, if there were no demarcations in this whole world, we did not belong to anybody, if only, and if only it was still Gondwanaland, we could have been living in harmony. It is only a wish and hope that the next generation will learn to live in harmony. So far, there are enough problems to cover the whole world. As you, all know "Christianity has not been tried and found wanting; it has been found difficult and not tried". This is a very hard theory for some people, scientifically we do take risks, but anything that has to do with the spiritual world we tend to be non-believer's. We rather seek refugee in our comfort zones of other solitude bodies.

As an observer from afar, I do not look for elements that are combustible that will create a fire if you rub them together. I suppose I am interested in the social structure within a given society and the set up of a multi cultural society. The world is changing and if you look at the margins you will find minority groups who have to bear the stigmata of the majority groups. I could not have hoped for anything better. The main reason I felt compelled to continue in prose was that I found it easier to describe certain political situation due to being there whilst it happened and also as they involved me personally. Being in Europe is not easy, and come rain come sunshine, home is always the best.

To everyone who is going to read this book I would like you to understand that after what happened to me, my experiences have led me to carry out research in anything that concerns Zimbabwe. Due to wanting the truth and finding out why we treat each other badly sometimes. It seems history repeat itself, some we have inherited the evilness from our ancestors. Others are the ones who can help their fellow citizens with all their hearts; they are always there for you when you need them.

In this case, my research, my personal interests have gone beyond my expectations. I have been trying to deliberate some of my sentiments about the dreams, which were shattered, but eventually this book is going to be something for the next generation to read and understand the atrocities that were suffered by their ancestors.

My dear friends *"**We lived, enjoyed Rhodesia and part of Zimbabwe**"*. Why I said this, I do not know, see you later! In my next issue! *"**Too hot to handle**"*

God bless all those Zimbabweans who are scattered in worldwide, colour, race or creed you are all people of the soil, you are Zimbabweans! Be proud to be one! Good luck!